SHE HAS NO PLACE IN PARADISE

Nawal El Saadawi was born in the village of Kafr Tahla in Egypt. She trained as a doctor of medicine and rose to become Egypt's Director of Public Health. She began writing thirty years ago, producing novels and short stories, and in 1972 published her first study of Arab women's problems and their struggle for liberation, *Women and Sex*. She has suffered at the hands of the Egyptian censors, being forced to shift publication of her works to Beirut, and earning her dismissal from the Ministry of Health. Along with other leading Egyptian intellectuals, she was imprisoned by Sadat. She writes in Arabic, but has published several books in English, including *Woman at Point Zero*, *The Hidden Face of Eve*, *Death of an Ex-Minister* and *The Fall of the Imam*. Nawal El Saadawi currently lives and works in Cairo.

SHE HAS NO PLACE IN PARADISE

Nawal El Saadawi

Translated by Shirley Eber

Minerva

A Minerva Paperback

SHE HAS NO PLACE IN PARADISE

First published in Great Britain 1987
by Methuen London
This Minerva edition published 1989
by Mandarin Paperbacks
Michelin House, 81 Fulham Road, London SW3 6RB

Minerva is an imprint of the Octopus Publishing Group

Copyright © 1987 by Nawal El Saadawi
Translation copyright © 1987 by Shirley Eber

A CIP catalogue record for this book
is available from the British Library
ISBN 0 7493 9063 8

Printed and bound in Great Britain by
Cox & Wyman Ltd, Reading

Contents

She was the Weaker

She was the Weaker

Only the middle finger of his right hand. No other finger would do. The little finger was longer than it should be, the thumb fatter. The nail of the index finger was dead; it had not grown after being squashed by a hoe. And the nail was important, maybe more important than the finger itself, for it was the nail that would open the way. He had implored his mother to be allowed to use something else, something harder, like the tip of a bamboo stick. But his mother poked him in the shoulder with her strong fingers and he rolled onto the ground, unable to spit but only to lick the earth with his tongue as he watched his mother's large feet steadily advancing, her lofty muscular body shaking the earth, her long hard fingers around the hoe, lifting it high as though it were a dry stick of corn, then bringing it down onto the earth to split it open like a watermelon.

As strong as an ox. On her head she carried loads

heavier than an ass. She kneaded troughs of dough, swept, cooked, hoed, carried children and gave birth, yet nothing about her grew tired or weary. But although she was his mother, who had created him from her flesh, from whose blood he had drunk, she had kept the strength for herself. He had inherited nothing from her but ugliness and weakness.

This violent urge to cling to his mother, to put his head on her breast and inhale the smell of her body was not love. He wanted to merge with her once more so that she could give birth to him anew with stronger muscles. He wanted to inhale some strength from her breath. When he kissed her, he didn't want to kiss but to bite her and eat her muscular flesh piece by piece. But he could not do it. All he could do was hide his head in her lap and hate her. Sometimes he would cry, sometimes he would run away. Once he stole away from the field at the end of the day and, with the hem of his *galabia*[1] between his teeth, he kept on running until he came to a place he did not know. Darkness surrounded him on all sides and he heard the distant howl of a wolf and turned on his heels and ran back home. And once he stole a five piastre piece from his mother's bag and took the Delta train to a village whose name he did not know. He began walking along its streets until his stomach rumbled and the soles of his feet burned. So he bought a ticket and took the train back to his village. Another time he stole a ten piastre piece and secretly went to the barber-surgeon. He stood before him panting.

– Speak up, lad. What d'you want?

He tried to dislodge his dry tongue from the roof of his mouth, hiding his hands in his *galabia*

– My fingers . . .
– What's wrong with them?
– They won't hold a hoe like my mother's do.
The man jabbed him in the shoulder:
– Shame on you, boy. Go and get your mother to feed you a pound of meat and you'll grow as strong as a horse.

He cried in his mother's ample lap until she bought him a piece of meat which he gobbled up. He drank and burped, feeling a pleasant warmth run through his fingers. He clenched them and stretched them, bent them and spread them, happy in his new-found power. But feeling his eyelids heavy, he closed his eyes and fell into a deep sleep. When he awoke two days later, he ran outside feeling that the remains of the meat had slipped away from inside him, together with the new-found power.

But there had to be a solution. In his head there was a brain at work. He was the cleverest man in the village. He read the newspapers to them, wrote letters for them, solved their problems, delivered the Friday sermon when the *Imam*[2] was away. But his brain and intelligence would not excuse him. For them, a real man meant having a strong body even if he had the mind of a mule.

His brain worked but his muscles were slack. Time passed. The fateful day was approaching and nothing he tried was of any avail. He locked the door of the back hall and exercised his muscles. He clenched his fingers, bent them and spread them and cracked them. Every night he exercised. At times his fingers clenched into a fist, at other times they would contort and then fall slack . . .

The day arrived. He watched his mother sweep and clean the hall before dawn and stack up wooden benches in front of the house. He pretended to be asleep or to be dead, but his mother poked him in the shoulder with those fingers of hers and he jumped to his feet. Groups of people began to fill the courtyard of the house; men carrying sticks, playing and dancing, women wearing gaily coloured robes, singing and ululating, throwing at him things which stung the nape of his neck. He was nailed to the ground by new slippers of yellow leather which chafed his feet. Around his neck was a new *kuffiya*³ at which he tugged with cramped fingers and with which he would have strangled himself had his muscles not been as soft as dough. His legs did not move but were pushed from behind, from the left, from the right, making him sway as though he were dancing with the dancers and reeling with the reelers . . . until he found himself at the threshold of the hall. Raising his head, he saw before him a curious thing, a thing the top half of which was covered in a large red shawl, the lower half, two thin bare legs, beside each leg a woman, grasping them with sturdy arms from which coarse veins bulged out.

He remained standing at the threshold, his eyes dazzled, his mouth trying to open to scream. But nothing emerged from between his lips except saliva which ran, warm and smooth, from the corner of his mouth, like the tail of a harmless snake . . .

He felt powerful fingers, like those of his mother, push him in the shoulder and sit him down. He felt somehow relieved with his buttocks on the washed damp ground. He remained seated, his eyes closed,

12

semi-conscious. But another thrust in his shoulder made him open his eyes to find himself face to face with the parted legs. He turned his face away and from the corner of his eye noticed a crowd of men and women behind him assembled in the courtyard, playing drums and flutes, dancing and standing waiting. Their eyes were wide open, eagerly and anxiously watching the door of the hall. No, he would not provide them with a scandal. He was not stupid. He was the cleverest man in the village . . . he read the newspapers and wrote letters for them, delivered the sermon when the *Imam* was away. He had to come out to them with his head held high, as all village men did, including the stupid boy who stammered and dribbled . . .

He stretched out his right hand and pushed his finger forward between the legs. But his arm trembled, violently shaking the finger which fell dangling like the tail of a dead puppy . . .

He did not stop. He kept trying and struggling. Copious sweat ran down the creases of his face and poured into his mouth; he licked it with his tongue, glancing furtively at the two women sitting beside him. Each of them was bearing down on a leg, faces turned away towards the wall, too polite to look at such a scene, or indifferent to something they'd seen many times, or declining to make themselves into inspectors of the virility of a man at his wedding ceremony, or embarrased or apprehensive, or something. What was important was they they did not see him.

Cautiously, he turned his eyes towards the door to find a section of the crowd standing and watching. From the corner of his eye, he noticed the old man, the father of the bride, standing at the door, his eyes darting back and forth from the door of the hall to the people's faces, anxious and fearful.

He rubbed his fingers confidently. No one knew the truth. The two women had seen nothing except the wall and the one it *did* concern was absorbed in worrying about his own honour . . .

No one knew the truth . . . except her. Her? Who? He did not know her, had never seen her, had seen neither her face nor her eyes nor even a single hair of her head. Now was the first time he was seeing her and he did not see a bride, did not see a person, but only a large red shawl at the end of which were two parted legs like those of a paralysed cow. But there she was in front of him, exposing his impotence. She stood up like a snare to entrap his weakness and failure and he hated her just as he hated his mother. He would have liked to tear her to shreds with his teeth or pour acid on her to burn her.

The hatred endowed him with wit and pride. He spat on the ground in displeasure and sucked his lips in contempt. He steeled himself, got up slowly from his place and turned towards the door, his head high, the handkerchief low. Striding slowly and surely towards the old man, he threw him a glance of superiority, then tossed the handkerchief in his face. It was as clean as before, as washed as before. Not one drop of red blood had stained it.

The eyes of the bride's father dropped in shame. His shoulders crumpled until his head was on his chest. Men surrounded him from all sides to comfort and support him, then they all turned to the door of the hall, at the ready . . .

14

The bride appeared at the threshold, her small head under the red shawl hanging in dejection, burning and accusing looks thrown at her from all sides . . .

[1] *galabia*: long loose robe commonly worn by Egyptian men and women
[2] *Imam*: Muslim prayer leader
[3] *kuffiya*: head-dress worn by Egyptian men

Tried and Recorded

Tried and Recorded

He was sitting on a seat, in front of him a large open file, his eyes unblinking. The walls of the large hall were white, the ceiling high with a crystal chandelier hanging from it. The table was covered with a green baize cloth, the cups of coffee forming a semi-circle on it, in the middle a larger cup containing a thick layer of coffee grounds, thicker than the other cups. The tumblers of iced water had condensed droplets of water on them. The air-conditioning buzzed in his ears like a busy bee; loud, raucous voices; heads nodding, circles on the walls, reflections of light on bald heads, nodding with them. In front of the largest cup with the thick layer of coffee grounds was a large body with a white head. When it moved to the right, all the heads moved to the right and, with them, the circles on the walls; then, when it moved to the left, all the heads moved to the left and, with them, the circles on the walls. Cigarette smoke rose into the air and coiled around the chandelier in small rings which were swallowed up by bigger ones.

As he was sitting on the seat, the name Medhat Abd al-Hamid struck his ears like a sharp stone. The lip wet with coffee moved, showing the tips of teeth yellowed with smoke. Medhat Abd al-Hamid is an exemplary fellow. The white head nodded and all the shiny bald heads nodded . . .

He tried to open his mouth, to move his tongue, but his lips would not part and his dry tongue would not budge. A strange bitterness stuck in his throat like glue. He knew the story of Medhat Abd al-Hamid; it was written in the file in front of him. But should he speak?

He moistened his lips with some iced water, feeling his throat rise and fall and scrape against the walls of his neck. What was the use of opening his mouth and saying something? They were not looking at him. Sometimes they spoke in a language he did not understand. Their hands were white, their fingernails smooth and clean, their collars starched stiff as cardboard. They laughed and exchanged jokes but he could not laugh, even though he laughed easily with his colleagues at the office and with his wife at home. But these people had bearing. Their looks ordered him silent and made him feel of a lower class.

But the name of Medhat Abd al-Hamid pierced his skull like a bullet. Medhat Abd al-Hamid was an explosion that shattered established rules. The moist lip and the shiny heads moved. Could he remain silent? He opened his lips to utter the words which were stuck in his throat like glue. The bitterness was absorbed deep inside and filled him and weighed on his stomach and chest so that he felt nauseous. But it was a futile nausea which was powerless to rid him of what he wanted to be rid of, a nausea which could only be cured by expelling the air from his chest and the blood from his heart, expelling the stuck words with them. But the air accumulated in his chest of its own accord and his heart took in and released blood, while his throat choked with words which stuck like a worm.

He half opened his mouth, letting out some hot breath. Could he get some words out? But what was the point of speaking? They were bigger than him. They controlled his means of livelihood. What was the use of launching into a losing battle? Of what use is a drop in the ocean? Who was he? The small patch in his trousers showed, his collar drooped, his hands were coarse and lined as they turned over the file. Of what use was the file?

What was the value of buried truth? Medhat *Bek*[1] Abd al-Hamid had stolen people's money, but his relative was influential. Abd al-Ghaffar *Effendi*[2] had discovered the theft, but he was only a junior clerk. The investigation began and dragged on and on. The prosecutor disappeared and another one came. Papers were lost and new ones appeared. The investigation ended and Abd al-Ghaffar *Effendi* ended up the robber.

He contemplated the large rings of smoke swallowing the small ones and relieved the bitterness in his throat with some water.

Could he defend Abd al-Ghaffar *Effendi*? He had promised him, before entering the hall, that he would defend him. But what was the use of defending? The large ate the small, in water, on land, in the air. If he did open his mouth and defend Abd al-Ghaffar *Effendi*, what then was the role of God?

He was only a second-grade civil servant, with a wife and nine children. Month after month he postponed buying a suit, his strength weakened with time and his trousers hung loose. And yet, how could he look Abd al-Ghaffar in the eye after the session? How could he look people in the eye? They were waiting for him behind the door of the hall for he had promised them to tell the truth. His hand shook in annoyance. Why did they ask miracles of him? He was no god. He shook his head in contempt. Of what use were those people anyway? They did not have control over his family's bread. The only things they had were reproachful and disparaging looks.

And what was the use of reproachful and disparaging looks? They would not snatch the bread from his mouth. Then again, why should he alone be the one to tell the truth? Why didn't they speak? Why didn't they shout? Why didn't they revolt? They were many, they were the majority, but they were dispersed and disunited. A thin stick of bamboo frightened them, a honeyed word pleased them.

He reached out for the cup of coffee and swallowed a sip. The name Abd al-Ghaffar *Effendi* came to his ears. As if it were a globule of spit, the moist lip spat out: The junior clerk who betrays his boss, this type can't be trusted, this type has no pedigree, this type is brought up in the alleyways.

The blood rushed to his head. What had alleyways to do with theft? He too had been brought up in alleyways. And he had no pedigree. Neither did he have relatives with important jobs nor a single influential one. But he had never stolen. It was thirty years since he'd been appointed in his job and he could

22

have stolen had he wanted. He had held other people's money and, when his youngest son became ill and he got into debt, the Devil had tempted him for a moment, but he took refuge in God and pushed the idea from his mind.

He asked himself why Medhat *Bek* Abd al-Hamid had stolen. He owned two cars and a building and only had two children. Perhaps, God forbid, he was sick. Or maybe he was just greedy.

The voices around him died down. He raised his head and saw the white head moving, the soft white hand holding a pen, writing the final verdict: Medhat Abd al-Hamid, innocent. His eyes were glued to the nib of the pen and he opened his mouth as if he were panting. He heard his own voice like a rattle: one minute, your honour.

The thick backs settled languidly into their leather chairs. Circles like smiles were drawn around the moist lips . . .

He put his hand in his pocket, took out a hand-kerchief and wiped off his sweat. He heard a coarse familiar voice say: write on it: tried and recorded.

---

[1] *Bek*: title of courtesy for one of high rank
[2] *Effendi*: title used for white-colour workers

Thirst

Thirst

The tarmac of the street beneath her feet had softened from the intensity of the sun's heat. It burned her like a piece of molten iron and made her hop here and there, bumping and colliding, unconsciously, like a small moth against the sides of a burning lamp. She could have made for the shade at the side of the street and sat for a time on the damp earth, but her shopping basket hung on her arm and her right hand clutched at a tattered fifty piastre note. She recited to herself the things she had to buy from the market so as to re-member them . . . half a kilo of meat at thirty-five piastres, a kilo of courgettes five piastres, a kilo of tomatoes seven piastres, three piastres change . . . half a kilo of meat at thirty-five piastres, a kilo of courgettes five piastres, a kilo of tomatoes seven piastres, three piastres change . . . half a kilo of meat . . .

She would have gone on repeating it until she got to

27

the market, as she did every day, but she suddenly noticed something strange, something absolutely incredible. Her surprise overcame the heat of the ground and she stopped and stared, her eyes wide, her mouth gaping. There was Hamida, flesh and blood, standing in front of a kiosk, in her hand a bottle of iced soft drink which she lifted to her lips and from which she was drinking.

At first glance, she didn't know it was Hamida. She had seen her from behind, standing in front of the kiosk, and never imagined it was Hamida. It was probably one of those girls whom she saw every day in front of the kiosk drinking soft drinks, respectable girls, who play with balls and skipping ropes and go to school and do not work in houses, girls like Suad and Mona and Amal and Mervat and all the friends of her young mistress Suhair.

She thought it was one of those girls and would have gone on her way, had she not noticed the shopping basket. She noticed it hanging from the girl's arm as she stood in front of the kiosk. She could not believe her eyes and, on closer examination, saw locks of curly hair hanging down the back of her head from beneath the white headscarf. That scarf was Hamida's, that arm from which hung a shopping basket hers. But could it really be Hamida?

She began to examine her closely from behind and saw the cracked heels sticking out of a pair of green plastic sandals. Those were indeed Hamida's sandals and her heels. But despite all that, she could not believe it and began to examine her from all sides, from the right, from the left, and each time she saw something which could only be Hamida's – her yellow linen

28

robe with a small tear on the side above her left breast, one tarnished earring in her right ear, the deep scar of an old wound on her right temple. It really was Hamida then, flesh and blood, and no other girl. She stood and studied her further . . .

Hamida was standing in front of the kiosk. In her right hand was a bottle of soft drink, on its surface translucent droplets of water. She was not drinking fast, like those other girls, but very very slowly. Her fingers clasped around the bottle to savour its coldness, she held on to it for a minute, then raised it slowly to her mouth, the edge of her lips making contact with the mouth of the bottle, licking it with her tongue to pick up all the dew around it. Then she lifted her arm a little to tilt the bottle gently into her mouth, only letting in one sip of the rose-coloured iced liquid. So far her lips kept strict control, holding the sip in her mouth for some time, not swallowing it in one go, but sucking it in slowly until the last drop had disappeared into her mouth, enjoying the utmost gratification, leaning her head backwards a little, the muscles of her back relaxing against the wall of the wooden kiosk . . .

She could no longer hold back. Without realizing it, she had gradually got closer to the kiosk and stood there, protected from the sun by its shade. Then she sat on the ground, her shopping basket by her side, her eyes glued to the sensuous meeting between Hamida's lips and the mouth of the bottle, then the sips and the slow sucking and the gratification and relaxation that followed. The ground was hot and burned her slender backside through the threadbare callico *galabia*. But she did not care. All she cared about was staying to watch, to follow Hamida's each and every movement.

She bent her head backwards whenever Hamida bent hers, opened her lips whenever Hamida opened hers, moved her tongue in her throat whenever Hamida moved her tongue . . . But her throat was parched, not one drop of saliva in it. Her tongue was dry and scraped against the walls of her throat like a wooden stick. The dryness stretched from her throat to her chest and plunged as far as her stomach. It was a strange awful dryness she had never felt before, as though water were suddenly evaporating from every cell of her body, from her eyes and nose and the skin which covered all of her, a dryness which reached her veins and the blood which ran though them. She felt a pain sear within her and felt that her skin was as thick, dry and coarse as that of a dried sardine. She had a salty taste in her mouth, as bitter as aloes, acrid and burning. She searched for some saliva with which to wet her salty lips, but the tip of her tongue burned without finding a drop. And Hamida was still in front of her, her lips around the mouth of the ice-cold bottle, each cell of her body absorbing the drink. Hamida carried a shopping basket just as she did; on her feet she wore sandals just like hers; on her body a cheap and torn *galabia* like her own; and she worked in houses as she did.

Her fingers holding the grubby fifty piastre note relaxed a little and the old record which she had memorized returned to her mind . . . half a kilo of meat at thirty five . . . kilo of courgettes at five piastres . . . kilo of tomatoes at seven piastres . . . leaves three piastres. The price of a bottle of soft drink was three piastres, very expensive. Last year it was only a tenth of the price. If this had happened a year ago, she could have considered buying a bottle. It was still not cheap, but she could have managed it. Sometimes, the courgettes were five and a half, the tomatoes seven and a half, the meat could never be more because the price was fixed. The lady of the house knew all the fixed prices by heart, so it was not possible to cheat her. Even the price of the vegetables, which changed daily, a bit more or a bit less, she knew day by day, as though she dreamed of prices at night. Supposing she were able to cheat on the price of the courgettes and the tomatoes, from where could she get the third piastre? It was not easy to claim that she had lost it since that game would not fool the fat lady with the hard slaps. She would also have to resort to lying and lying was the brother of theft, as her mother had told her. Do not, my daughter Fatima, lay your hand on a single piastre. Theft, my daughter, is a sin and God will burn you in the fire of hell . . .

She was frightened of fire, of it burning her hair and head and body. If a match could hurt her so, how much more would fire burn her whole body? She could not imagine such a fire, had neither known nor felt it. What she did feel was that other sort of fire which burned her insides, the fire of dryness and of thirst, a fire which nothing could quench other than a few sips from a bottle of soft drink. The kiosk beside her, she could touch its walls with her shoulder. And Hamida in front of her was drinking a bottle of soft drink. But how could she get three piastres? The easiest way was to spread them equally over the price of the meat, the courgettes and the tomatoes, adding one piastre to each. Her mother's words had no meaning for her now. The fire with which she had threatened her she did not know, and she had never seen anyone burned by it. Perhaps this fire did not exist. And if it did, it was very far away from her, as far away as death. She did not know when she would die, did not even imagine she could die some day.

She got up, shook the dust from her *galabia* and stood watching Hamida as she emptied the last gulp into her mouth, pursing her lips around the bottle and not wanting to let go. As the man pulled the bottle from her hand, she gave it a long parting kiss before it was gone from between her lips for ever. Then she opened her left hand carefully and counted out three whole piastres . . .

She trembled a little as she stood in the same place in front of the kiosk where Hamida had stood. A waft of humid air came from inside the kiosk, carrying with it the smell of soft drink. Come what may after this. The hard slaps no longer hurt her for she had grown used to them. The fire which burned no longer frightened her for it was far away. The world and all the pain and fear it contained were nothing compared to one sip of ice-cold soft drink.

The Article

The Article

The red blood rose quietly to his cheeks and raced to his fingers and toes, warm and filling with the warmth of the blazing fire in the heart of the large stove, whilst the cold pen between his heat-reddened fingers hovered over the white sheet of paper, moving to and fro on its empty lines, producing nothing except short squiggles.

He got up from his desk, went over to the stove and squatted down in front of it, bringing the pen close to let the warmth spread through its cold body. The burning flames of the fire held him spellbound and he stared fixedly into it, feeling a strange lethargy, like intoxication or something even more pleasurable. Secretly he'd have loved to go on squatting like this for the rest of his life, beside that delicious warmth which ran through every joint in his body. But the pen between his fingers reminded him of the article which he had to submit to the newspaper that same day. So, summoning up his will-power, he returned sluggishly to the seat at his desk. He put pen to paper and tried to write. But the nib of his pen once again began hovering over the white page, drawing short squiggly lines like the legs of cockroaches.

Instantly, his memory darted back to himself as a child sitting in a biology lesson drawing the feelers and legs of a cockroach. He had hated cockroaches and biology classes and would have liked to jump over the wall and run away from school. But his father's eyes, looking at him from over a plate of spinach, were saying imploringly: Study, my boy, so that you can become a man of great importance like your uncle, the *bek*. The image of his uncle leapt before him: getting out of his long black car, together with his fat white wife, behind them their elegant daughter, the three of them walking to their house built of red bricks, looking contemptuously at the children gathered around the car, putting white silk handkerchiefs to their noses to protect themselves from the dust storm of the unpaved alleys. He heard a child sigh and whisper in his ear: Your uncle, the *bek*!

He had responded with a look of great pride, then ran towards his uncle, holding out a hand dirty with mud and breathlessly saying to him: Welcome home, uncle!

The pen fell from between his fingers and hit the desk. He smiled to himself cynically, studying the cockroach legs on the paper which had dragged these images back from the distant past, and wiped his nose with his soft silken handkerchief to let the expensive manly perfume drive out the ghosts of the dusty past. Looking up from the desk to gaze at the sumptuous pictures hanging on the wall, his eyes fell on the large face of his wife and his heart contracted as he studied the icy sharp features: the nose tilted upward in disdain, the thin taut lips which he did not know how to kiss, the sharp piercing eyes whose blueness was tinged with a repulsive and haughty arrogance. He chewed his lips, wondering what good outward appearances were in marriage and what use Khadija's beautiful features were to him. His eyes turned away from those of his wife and fell on the paper. He picked up the pen to write the title of the article and in large letters on the top of the page he wrote: Our Path to Socialism. He drew a thick line under it, then began thinking about the start of the article. His fingers grasped the pen, pressing as if to squeeze the words out of it. But the pen wriggled and squirmed on the paper, either drawing lines under the title or cockroach legs, whilst the fingers of his other hand toyed with his beard or moustache, now pulling out a hair, now groping for a crevice . . .

He craned his neck forwards, shook the pen lightly and put the nib on the paper; but realizing that, with all the lines and cockroach legs on it, the paper was no longer any good for the article, he crumpled it up and threw it into the wastepaper basket. Opening the drawer of the desk to take out a new sheet, his eyes fell on a small book entitled *Towards Socialism* which he picked up. He opened it quickly and his eyes sparkled as he read, feeling that revelation and inspiration were pouring out of it. He closed the book, tossed it back into the drawer, took out another piece of clean white paper and fell over it writing: I am a *fellah*, the son of a poor *fellah* . . .

He raised the pen from the paper to see how the

sentence looked. The word 'poor' did not please him so he crossed it out and wrote the word 'destitute'. He smiled in pleasure as he read: . . . the son of a destitute *fellah*. Yes, that word was better, proving to people that he was a man with an honourable past.

Burning with enthusiasm, the pen flowing on the paper brought to his mind the boundless glory of poverty and bestowed on his grandfathers and father the limitless pride of deprivation and want. The fervour of his enthusiasm unconsciously lifted the lid off the store of painful memories lying deep in his brain. From beneath it, images hidden unawares in his unconscious began to steal in: his mother in her dusty black *galabia*, her black headcloth, the long end wrapped around a number of corncobs, her swollen cracked feet beneath a metal anklet shuffling heavily and slowly like the hoofs of an exhausted camel, whilst he, in his grimy worn-out *galabia*, ran his fingers through the ashes in the oven, his spindly knees under his chest, his father's choking voice ringing in his ears: 'He works in the field with me', his mother's weary voice saying: 'No, he'll go to school.' Then her mouth gaped in a yawn, her upper lip revealing her protruding teeth and a large expanse of red gums. Immediately there appeared before him the protruding teeth and red gums of his uncle, yawning when he saw him crouched in the corner of the large sitting room, thin knees gripping the hem of his ragged trousers, dry lips clenched against the rumbling of his empty stomach. His uncle's yawns increased as the aroma of food wafted in from the kitchen, as did the rumbling of his stomach. He turned his face away, feigning indifference to his uncle's mouth whilst at heart he carried an unbounded hatred for this uncle who sat on a soft sofa yawning like a prize bull . . . and for his uncle's wife who took her time coming out of the kitchen to call him to supper, her legs rubbing together as she walked, like a pregnant cow; and for his stupid father who was good for nothing other than hoeing the soil; and for his mother who had carried him in her rumbling stomach and had bequeathed him only ugliness and poverty; and for all those people who slept on beds and went to school and paid their expenses and, after all that, still had enough left to eat until they were satiated.

He hated everything . . . memories, school, students, winter, the cold wind which blew on him all night long through the cracks in the walls; and he hated the daytime and the sun which burned his head all summer long, the caretaker who demanded the rent for his room every month, the tenants who lived in proper flats, the thin dark woman who lived in the wooden room on the other side of the roof, the smell of her clothes mixed with the smell of stale cooking, her cold hiss under his neck as she whispered shameful words in his ear.

He hated everything, even himself, and the rotten, stagnant smell in his clothes, and his stubborn body which always oozed that sticky sweat, his knobbly toes which stuck out of his shoes, the looks of hatred which always appeared in his eyes in the small cracked mirror . . . and his greedy stomach which devoured, in one fleeting moment, a loaf of bread and ten balls of *ta'amia*,[1] then shrivelled up empty and growled like a wolf.

He hated anything and everything except for that

strange and wondrous moment when he curled up with his bread and ten *ta'amia* balls and sniffed them and licked them with his tongue, then put them in his mouth and chewed them thoroughly until they dissolved deep inside him and disappeared . . .

His lips parted without his being aware of it and a tiny droplet of warm saliva which he couldn't feel with the tip of his tongue escaped from between them and dripped onto the page. Noticing it, he sucked his lips contemptuously, reading the words 'poverty' and 'want' which he had written. He crumpled up the paper in his hand and threw it into the wastepaper basket, then took out a clean sheet of paper and, with heavy heart, wrote: Socialism is wind not coming in through cracks in the wall all night, the sun not falling on heads throughout the day, toes not sticking out of shoes, hatred not accumulating inside people's hearts . . .

The pen between his fingers stopped. He looked at the last sentence, read it and meditated on it . . . hatred not piling up inside people's hearts. He asked himself what people would fight with if hatred did not pile up inside them. What, other than hatred, had taught him to fight and be determined to succeed? What, other than hatred, kindled his will, drove away sleep, checked his natural instincts and deprived every cell of his mind and body of rest, even for one passing moment? What else, other than hatred? He reached out, crumpled up the paper, threw it in the wastepaper bin and took out a clean sheet . . .

But his pen once again began to hover over the empty lines, putting down doodles or returning to its original pastime of drawing cockroach legs. The words

40

did not want to come out, as if he had never written before. But he had done, often. He'd often filled pages in magazines and newspapers. He had put one word after the next, one sentence after the next. It had never been hard for him. His name was long and filled the width of the page. He had a broad education which ran from primary school to a master's degree in law. He had memorized a great number of intellectual words and new expressions. He craned his neck forward in readiness and confidence, amazed at how all this time was being wasted in writing simple conventional words which anyone without the education that he had and who hadn't memorized all the expressions that he had memorized, could write.

His fingers folded around the pen confidently and he pressed it against the paper and wrote: The re-volutionary phase through which we are now passing calls for the integration of fundamental and essential ideology with practical work within the framework of public laws in a world heading towards the horizons of a socialist future.

He put his pen on the desk and wiped the tip of his nose with the silk handkerchief imbued with the scent of expensive man's perfume. He studied the words he had written, stretching his neck forwards in pride. He yawned, spreading his legs and arms, and stretched in relaxation. He looked at the clock, then folded the paper quickly and put it in his pocket. He went out into the street and saw the young boy run to the long car to open the door. He got in and sat down to turn on the ignition. He saw the small boy eagerly polish the car window, then stand in the middle of the road checking for a gap in the passing traffic. Then he signalled to him to move, coming towards him, his hand outstretched. He pressed hard on the accelerator and the car shot forward like an arrow into the wide street . . .

In the small mirror in front of him, he saw the small boy step back, his hand still outstretched, in his eyes a look he recognized . . . a look which for many long years had stared back at him from the small cracked mirror.

[1] *ta'amia*: an Egyptian national dish of spiced, deep-fried rissoles made from dried white broad beans.

Ring of
Revolving Horses

Ring of
Revolving Horses

The similarity between herself and the horses was great, but she raised her two front legs up high so that it looked as though she were turning on her hind ones. One of them was in the middle. Why him in particular in the middle? He was no different from her . . . the two forelegs raised up high, not touching the ground, but lifted above the knees and hanging down by the side like hands. He was exactly like her. But he was in the middle, in the centre of the circle. No one came near him. Everyone revolved in the outer circumference. His face was turned towards himself, looking without blinking. He stood when he liked, turned when he liked, shook a leg when he liked, stamped a hoof when he liked, and leaned to the right or to the left when he liked.

The spectators were sitting in their seats, the back rows seeing the backs of those in front, those in front seeing the backs of the horses. Everyone saw only backs, backs which were hunched to reveal the vertebrae so clear and sharp it hurt the eyes to look. The circular movement was also painful to the eyes and the wooden seats hurt the thighs. The arena was large, wide and round and had no walls to keep out the cold air.

The cold air chased away sleep. The spectators blew into their hands to warm them. The hoofs struck the ground, the regular sound following the movement, the movement in the form of a circle. Everyone in the outer circumference, one alone in the middle, one alone, no different from the rest, the front legs raised up high, hanging ineffectually down to the stomach. Only the two hind legs turned, just like a horse dancing or kicking. But she was no horse. The faces were turned towards the middle, the backs towards the spectators. And the spectators grew weary of the sight of backs and would have been overcome by sleep on the wooden seats had it not been for the cold air which lashed them.

The Picture

The Picture

Everything in Nirjis' life could have gone on in the
same way, had her hand not accidentally fallen on
Nabawiya's back and had her fingers not hit upon a
soft ball of flesh. Astonished, she watched two small
bulges quiver under her *galabia* with the shaking of
her arms as she did the washing at the sink. It was the
first time she discovered that Nabawiya had buttocks.
Nabawiya who had come to them from the village the
previous year, the small servant with a body as thin
and dry as a stick of corn. You almost couldn't have
told her front from her back and, if her name hadn't
been Nabawiya, you could have taken her for a boy . . .

Nirjis found herself in front of the mirror in her
room. She turned herself around. Her eyes widened in
surprise to see two small bulges quivering under her
dress. She put out a hand to examine her back and her
shaking fingers came across two soft balls of flesh . . .
she too was developing buttocks!

49

She lifted up her dress from behind to uncover them, twisting her head to see them from the other side. But they turned with her body and disappeared behind her. She tried to keep the lower half of her body still before the mirror and to turn her head, but she could not do it. As her head turned, so did the upper part of her body; and whenever the top half turned, so did the bottom. She was somewhat astonished that she could not see herself from behind whereas she could see Nabawiya. It seemed to her at that moment that she had discovered a new human affliction: not to be able to see the body one was born with and which one carried everywhere and always, as one could see the bodies of others.

It occurred to her to go to the kitchen and ask Nabawiya to look at her back and describe her buttocks to her. What shape were they? Were they round? Or egg-shaped? Did they quiver as she sat or only when she walked? Did they stick out and attract attention or not?

She was about to go, but stopped. Could she ask Nabawiya such a thing? Nabawiya was a servant with whom she did not converse. She issued her with orders which were far from conversation, to which Nabawiya's replies of 'Very well' or 'Yes' were far from answers but rather automatic and regular responses delivered at exactly the same speed and the same pitch as the oscillations of a machine.

She felt frustrated and determined to see her back by herself. So she pulled up her dress to be completely naked from behind, planted her feet firmly on the ground and twisted her head, turning her eyes to the back of her body. But her head could soon move no further and her eyes could not complete the circle around her. She tensed her muscles and tried again. Whilst she was turning her head in front of the mirror with her back completely naked, she suddenly saw her father's eyes and trembled. Although she knew they weren't really his eyes but those of his photo hanging on the wall, her small body continued to tremble until she pulled down the dress and covered her back. She could not take her eyes off his but wanted to see them. Every time she looked at her father, she felt she wasn't seeing enough of him and wanted to see more. Thirteen years since she was born and every day she saw him only from the back. When his back was turned towards her, she could raise her eyes and gaze at his tall, broad frame. But she had never once raised her eyes to his and it had never happened that she had exchanged glances or words with him. If he looked at her, she would bow her head; if he spoke to her, it wasn't conversation but rather directions or orders to which she replied 'Very well' or 'Yes' in mechanical allegiance and blind obedience. When he had ordered her to leave school and stay at home, she left school and stayed at home. When he ordered her not to open the windows, she did not open the windows. When he ordered her not to look out from behind the shutters, she did not look out from behind them. Even when he ordered her to wash and pray before going to sleep so as to dream only honourable dreams, she washed herself and prayed and dreamed only honourable dreams.

Her eyes remained fastened on his. She wanted to look at him and not bow her head, to fix her eyes on his eyes, to see them, know them, become familiar with them. But she was unable to do so. There was always a distance separating her eyes from his and she could not see them close up, even though her nose almost touched the picture. His face appeared large to her, his nose huge and curved, his eyes sunken and wide-set, almost swallowing her. She hid her face in her hands. She recalled the large desk from behind which her father's curved nose rose above a pile of papers. From time to time he inspected the long queue of people standing in front of him, their eyes fixed on him, pleading and humble. His large head shook amongst the piles of papers and his long coarse fingers held a pen which he ran across the papers at great speed. She pressed her thin legs together as she sat in the corner, withdrawn into herself, holding her breath. Could she really be the daughter of such a great man? When her father stood up, his tall, broad frame towered behind the desk so that the tip of his nose almost touched the ceiling. She raised her head proudly as she walked alongside him in the street, all eyes on her father. All mouths that opened did so in supplication to her father; her small ears could almost catch the whispers of people in the street: That's the big man himself and that's his daughter Nirjis walking by his side! When they crossed the street and her father held her hand in his and wrapped his large fingers around her small ones, her heart thumped, her breathing raced and she bent her head to kiss his hand. The moment her lips brushed his large hairy hand, a strong smell entered her nose . . . that distinctive smell of her father. She didn't know exactly what it was, but she could smell it everywhere he was. When he came into her room, she could smell it all over the room, in the bed, in the cupboard, in her clothes. Sometimes she would bury her head in his clothes, even kiss them, so as to smell it more, and kneel before the large picture of him above the bed in what was almost prayer – not that normal prayer which one performs quickly to a god one has never seen, but rather the real worship of a real god whom she saw with her own eyes, heard with her own ears and smelled with her own nose. It was he who bought her food and clothes, who had a large office and a mass of papers and knew everything in them, who satisfied people's needs and, above all, who wrote with a pen at dazzling speed.

Nirjis found herself kneeling in front of the picture as though praying. She got up, her head bowed in humility, and kissed his hand as she usually did every night before going to sleep . . . Lying on her back, her prominent buttocks came into contact with the bed and a new and delicious tremor ran through her body. She put out her trembling hand to feel her back. Two rounded mounds of flesh were squeezed between herself and the bed. She turned over to stop herself feeling them and sleep, but her raised buttocks pressed down onto her stomach. She rolled onto her side, but they remained touching the bed with every breathing movement. She held her breath for a moment, but it soon started up again in quick pants, making her small body shudder, shaking the bed which squeaked slightly. It seemed to her, in the silence of the night, that it must be audible and that it must have reached the ears of her father sleeping in his room who would certainly know where it came from and why.

She trembled at the thought and tried to control her breathing to stop the bed squeaking and would have

53

choked had air not forcibly entered her chest. Her body shook violently, as did the bed, screeching in the silence of the night with a coarse sound. She jumped out of bed . . .

When her feet hit the floor, the bed stopped squeaking and she could hear only the sound of her rapid breathing, which gradually began to quieten down. When silence returned to her room, she remembered that she hadn't washed for prayer before going to bed. She was relieved to discover that this was the reason for the sinful feelings which had crept into her impure body.

Whilst Nirjis was standing in front of the sink performing the ritual cleansing and praying, she heard a faint sound coming from behind the kitchen door. Nabawiya still wasn't asleep? She pushed the door gently, but it would not open. She heard the sound again and, putting her ear to the door, heard clearly the sound of rapid breathing and commotion. She smiled, feeling somewhat relieved. Nabawiya was awake like her, discovering her new buttocks! Her head still against the door, she put her eye to the keyhole and looked into the kitchen. The small sofa on which Nabawiya slept was empty and she saw something move on the kitchen floor. She looked again. The pupils of her eyes widened as they fixed on the naked mound of flesh with two heads, rolling on the floor. One of the heads was Nabawiya's with its long plaits. The other was the head of her father with its long curved nose! At that moment she could have fallen to the ground, but her eyes were fixed to the keyhole as though they were a part of it, her sight frozen onto that large naked mound as it rolled,

54

Nabawiya's head on the floor banging against the trashcan, her father's head lifted up above, knocking against the underside of the sink. But they quickly swapped positions and then Nabawiya's head was banging against the sink, her father's head beside the trashcan . . . Then the two heads almost disappeared under the shelf which held the cooking pots so that she could only see four legs and twenty toes, shuddering with rapid quivers and intertwining with each other in a curious way, resembling a sea animal with numerous arms or an octopus.

Nirjis did not know how she dislodged her eye from the keyhole, nor how she returned to her room, where she looked in the mirror. Her small head was shaking and spinning. Her tired eyes caught a glance of her rounded buttocks which shook with the shuddering of her body. As she put out her hand, unaware, to uncover her back completely, she caught sight of her father's face. The old trembling almost ran down her arm to make her pull down her dress and cover herself; but her arm did not move. She kept on staring into her father's face without bowing her head. His eyes were open wide and bulging, his sharp curved nose dividing his face into two. A long cobweb, quivering with the night breeze rushing in through the shutters, had attached itself to the tip of his nose.

Nirjis went up to the picture to blow the cobweb off her father's face. But a shower of her saliva spattered the picture and stuck the cobweb to her father's face. She tried once again to blow it off, but it only stuck more. Unconsciously, she stretched out her hand and with her long sharp fingernails tried to remove the long silken thread from the picture. She did actually manage to remove it, but with it she removed the paper of the picture which was wet with her saliva and which fell from her fingers to the ground in small pieces . . .

But He was No Mule

But He was No Mule

He hadn't lost consciousness, was aware of everything going on around him. He could see and hear voices clearly and sharply, perhaps more clearly than at any other time. But he did not move, did not seem to be breathing, for his chest appeared neither to rise nor fall. And in fact, his chest did not rise or fall. But secretly he was breathing. How could he breathe in secret? How was it possible for his lungs to inhale and exhale air with no movement or sound? How could air enter and leave his chest without the tiny hairs in his nostrils moving? Nobody knows, not even he himself. He had started doing many things without knowing how. Some of his limbs had acquired a strange new power, naturally, unconsciously, without training. In one day, he had learned how to scale the high wall, to leap up in one mighty bound that lifted him up to the small iron skylight onto which he held with all his strength, raising his body up with the muscles of his hand to look out from between the bars at that miraculous small square of sky.

How did his body stretch and contract, harden and relax, appear and disappear according to certain sounds or glances or signals? Indeed, how could a new limb grow out of him, like an amoeba or a single-cell animal, whenever necessary? Who would have believed that this body, which he had carried around for over twenty years and whose weight, density and powers he knew, could change in such a way and at such a speed, as if it were not his body at all? How many times he had put a folded letter between his gums and inner lip, looking in front as he passed by the guard, with all his will-power and all his instincts of survival willing him not to see . . . and he didn't see.

It was not strange, therefore, that he breathed with his chest still, that he inhaled air without the hairs of his nostrils moving. This was the only way of keeping himself alive. For as soon as his chest stopped moving and the hairs of his nostrils stopped quivering, that harsh sound ringing through the air also stopped and then landed on something solid which had the softness of flesh and had certain sensations which he felt and knew. It was not agonizing pain, wasn't even pain at all, but was more like a kind of pushing or pulling. Here too the body acquires a curious and extraordinary force, becomes immune to pain, as if the coarse stick which was raised into the air and then fell, did not strike *his* body, but a body separate from, yet close to, his own: so close it may not have been separate at all but may actually have been his. With this doubt, ambiguity and confusion, the pain too became something so dubious and ambiguous that it was tinged with other feelings resembling joy or pleasure. He almost felt happy. He had an urge to smile when the strange thought crossed his mind that the sergeant was the only one panting from tiredness. He stood a step away from him, rubbing his hand from all the pain he felt after so much effort, letting out a faint sigh mixed with his panting breath. He himself smiled inwardly, without moving his lips, watched the sergeant without moving his chest, in that infernal way, no description of which is to be found in medical books. How ignorant doctors are of the human body. They describe it as a piece of flesh controlled by five ineffectual senses. Do they know anything about those new senses or limbs which grow suddenly? And how could they know since they had not lived through the un-ique experience he was living?

He saw the sergeant straighten up, flex his muscles, brandish the cane in front of him, hit its head against his hand and raise the other hand with fingers clenched, to strike him on the forehead. Officer Alawi was short, fat and white, his upper lip cleaved in the centre to form a canal between his mouth and nose, just like a foetus in its first months when those partitions that separate the members of the body from each other are not yet complete. The strange voice rang in his ears; he couldn't tell if it was coming from the nose or from the mouth: Where's the printing press, you numbskull? Talk! What will silence gain you? All his strength and resistance flowed into his lips, leaving his body slack, loose, outstretched. His lips formed themselves into two thin hard lines which he clamped shut with all his might.

The sharp nasal voice rang in his head. He was

incapable of talking. Not from lack of desire or because he had lost the power to move his tongue; nor because he had lost his memory and had forgotten where the printing press was; nor because he was sticking to some principle or promise or commitment, for he no longer remembered such human matters and emotions. Indeed, he was no longer human. He had become another being, with another body, other limbs. He was capable of talking, capable of opening his mouth and saying: High Street, number six. These words were still clear in his memory, clearer than anything else. No, there was almost nothing else in his memory. He had forgotten everything: the number of his house, the name of his street, how his mother looked, the science of geology which he had spent years of his life studying. His memory had emptied of all content and nothing remained except those few words: High Street, number six.

The sharp nasal voice echoed in his head, creating strange reverberations in its cavity which swelled and expanded as if it were a large empty chamber which amplified sound like a microphone.

Where's the printing press, you numbskull. Talk! What will silence gain you? Officer Alawi with the hare-lip could not know what silence would gain him, other than that beating so intense it verged on death or perhaps really was death. But there was something else Alawi did not know, could not know – not because of some brain deficiency nor because some of his facial cells had stopped growing at an early foetal stage, but because it was something so strange that nobody had ever known it; and he himself would not have known it were he not now living this amazing moment, a moment when the body separates from the self with neither of the two dying, a moment when your body seems far from your self, not very far, but separate from it by a minute distance, one single hair's breadth. At such a moment, your body does not concern you, for it is not your body, its pain not your pain, its survival not your survival. At that moment, in that fraction of a moment, the survival instinct is split into two unequal parts. One part, which is very large, you imagine to be the whole, that there is no other part. But it is not far away, not far at all, as near as that body is to you. And thus this amazing thing happens. You withdraw into your self, form a shell around it and are filled with all the survival instinct you possess. Your body is there, not far away from you, naked, limp and outstretched, feeling neither heat nor cold, unable to differentiate blows from kicks, from pokes, from jabs. Everything has become the same to it, like a pressure which comes and goes, goes and comes, like the natural pressure, on any being or body, of the atmosphere from above and of the earth from below.

At such a moment, the survival of that body has no meaning. To survive or not to survive are one and the same. What is important is your self, that gelatinous, tangible yet intangible point which constitutes your survival, that unknown, secret drop of life which makes you live even if you have lost the feeling that your body exists, a drop which, were it to dry up, would cause the life within you to dry up and you would die, even if your body were still tangible.

It is not surprising that the survival instinct should be concentrated in this drop, that he should curl up and form a hard impermeable shell around it, like a snail of iron whose mouth is strangely shut, as if its iron lips had melted away and dissolved into each other so that no mouth or even a sign of one any longer existed. But could Officer Alawi with the foetal lip imagine all this? Could he picture that iron snail without a mouth within which is a minute space which holds no more than one drop in which all his life and all his shaken-out memory are dissolved, one drop distilled and concentrated into one thing: the printing press.

Where is the printing press, you numbskull. Talk! What will silence gain you?. . . The nasal voice still repeated the stupid, hollow question. What will silence gain you? A strange question, the strangest he'd ever heard, a question to which there is no answer, a question that the whole of the human race, which has answered millions of questions and discovered millions of the universe's secrets, has never to this day been able to answer. A question without an answer, the question itself not a question, a question no one knows how to ask nor what he is asking nor what exactly it is he wants to know. For he knows the answer: not that clear common knowledge which can be known but an unknown knowledge which is exactly like lack of knowledge. He knows that there is a small core in a place within him in which life is concentrated, like a focal point, small, precise and invisible and which is perhaps not there at all, but tangible nevertheless in some place in his body. No, not his body, but in some place in his self which he knows and feels to no avail, like a mirage which is no mirage but reality represented in his being, a reality as minute as one tiny atom of which he is aware every moment and which he preserves inside himself and curls up around, clinging on to it for eternity. For it is the secret of his life, existence and survival, which he knows as well as he knows himself and is as ignorant of as he is ignorant of himself.

Where is the printing press? Talk, you numbskull! What will silence gain you? . . . The sharp nasal voice became sharper and more nasal. The shell around him grew thicker and harder. The drop inside himself grew safer and surer, pure, refined and so transparent that the letters could almost be seen clearly through it! High Street, number six. Letters shining the colour of lead, intertwined and interlaced, growing thicker and thinner, separating and meeting. The smell of paper pulverized between the clogs of the press, a strong strange smell which does not enter through the nostrils like other smells, but which splits the bones of your skull and assaults your brain with a word which you know even before you read it. The press turns in your head, the lead letters chatter together like teeth and the word is born. It is only a word and nothing but a word, yet it is the point at which all things begin, the point at which his life began and stretched throughout the years until this moment which he was now living, a long thread beginning at a point and stretching up to that gelatinous minute point around which his self was wrapped, enclosed and protected like a foetus in its mother's womb.

Now it became less blurred. He was able to picture a long thread, as fine as a hair, which began at a point around which turned the press in High Street, number six and which ended at that point imprisoned within himself in that wide barren desert where there was nothing except the sergeant and his cane with its thick curved head and Officer Alawi with his sharp nasal voice.

Where is the press, you numbskull. Talk! What will silence gain you?

The question was the same but the answer was no longer unknown. He could not say that he knew the answer or that it was possible for him to say why he was silent or what good it would do him or what the significance of that long thread stretched between two points of unknown origin was, one of which he himself imposed, the other which was imposed on him as his self was imposed. But he was absolutely certain that the printing press still turned in that small apartment in High Street. Its clogs turned, its lead letters chattered, the paper pounded between its teeth and the strong smell penetrated the brain. Could they discover where it was from the smell? Could they stop the press turning? Could they gouge out that eye with which he saw despite the vast distances between his place in the desert and its place in High Street? Could they erase that first point at which the long thread of his life began and from which it stretched to the point of his life imprisoned within himself?

Could the smell come out? Could one open one's mouth to inhale or gasp or yawn and would the words High Street, number six, escape from between one's lips with the air? Could that happen? The mere thought of the possibility of it happening wracked his being, for his being was one of the two points between which the thread was stretched and his survival was the survival of that thread stretched between two points, the two together, since the disappearance of one meant breaking the thread and the disappearance of the other.

Where is the printing press, you numbskull? Talk! What will silence gain you?

Only now could he understand why he kept silent, why he did not open his clamped lips and yawn, to let out the words High Street, number six, with the air. It was not a matter of sticking to a principle or keeping a promise to others, for here others had no existence. His body was closer to him than others, was itself separate from his self by only a hair's breadth. He no longer existed, so what did others matter? But the issue was far more important than that. It was a matter of his self, of his essence, the survival or non-survival of this essence, the continuation and presence of this stretched thread carrying water and air from High Street to his essence imprisoned within the shell. To survive or not to survive was the issue. Survival here was not physical survival since the body no longer had feelings, but was survival of another kind. It was the survival of that thread stretched between those two points. What was that thread and what were those two points? That he did not know at all.

He no longer heard the sharp nasal voice. No doubt Officer Alawi had grown silent for a while to rest his vocal cords. He began to hear the heavy feet of the sergeant, steel striking the cement floor. He heard the sound of the cane raised in the air, rest a moment, then fall suddenly and hit something solid with soft flesh and density; but it was not flesh, or at least not *his* flesh, rather the flesh of another, not very far from him, perhaps separate from him by only a minute hair's breadth, yet a distance nonetheless, separating him from that beaten flesh. If he were a mule, he'd have died; but he was no mule. He was a person with a mind which knew how to think, how to overcome any force, how to win in the end. How to win . . . how.

He was only one imprisoned point, not free-floating in the air. He could not break free and explode like an atom, but was imprisoned inside a thick hard shell without a mouth. How to win, with what force, what enormous, crushing, destructive force? He could scarcely believe in such power, could hardly contain his joy or hide his pride. And what pride! He was capable of winning, despite everything. Capable of closing his mouth and not talking. Capable of letting the press turn and turn. Capable of making life run in a long thread stretched between High Street and his remote place in the desert. He was the winner. He was happy. He almost wanted to dance.

There was the nasal voice once again. There *he* was, clamping his iron lips together into one lip. If they prised his mouth open with a saw, not one atom of air would escape from his throat since it too was blocked and had no opening. And because he had learned how to breathe inside the shell without air entering or leaving.

What did silence gain you, you numbskull? Your colleague confessed. High Street, number six. It was the sharp nasal voice. Him, with the nose open onto his mouth. Him, who said High Street, number six. Him, the sharp nasal one.

He didn't know exactly what happened. But the voice rang in his ears like an explosion, like a large inflated balloon bursting, like a long thin stretched wire cut suddenly. He no longer saw the sergeant, no longer heard the sharp nasal voice. He no longer saw or heard anything. He did not feel the coarse fingers of the sergeant close around his feet and drag him off, no one knows where.

The Lie

The Lie

Suddenly, he was stark naked.

He did not know how he'd taken his clothes off, but he wanted to present her with a fait accompli, with a naked man. Nakedness in itself was a guarantee that the relationship between them would develop. He had no patience left. The present was fraught with danger and the future uncertain. He no longer had time, for youth was slipping away, middle age fast approaching as he neared forty. His reserves of strength were waning and his body often failed him at moments when the heart was aflame.

He was talking about something or other. The subject was dry. Perhaps scientific or political or philosophical. She was sitting in front of him, wearing a fashionable dress. Her expression was neither provocative nor seductive nor did it contain any hint of that lustfulness which modest women learn to perfect. On the contrary, her expression repelled rather than attracted a man.

Repelled him utterly and irrevocably, as one would repel sickness or death or something which one feels would be impossible to get rid of once it took hold.

We are all heading for death whether we like it or not, he said to himself as he caught sight of himself naked in the mirror. Twenty years he had lived with the mother of his five children, a respectable, bashful and virginal wife who made love without undressing.

As he turned away from the mirror, he caught sight of a chest as hairy as a monkey's and a stomach as protruding as a pregnant woman's. He hadn't thought his stomach was that big. It grew a little each day, imperceptibly, and his trousers got a little tighter, no more than a half millimetre or so. But it all accumulated. The days accumulated, tens, hundreds, thousands and with them the millimetres, one by one, for twenty years.

She was sitting, a book in her hand. She knew he was sitting in his chair, talking, utterly dignified. The words flowed from his mouth one by one without pause or silence, as though he was chewing his saliva and then excreting sprawling inseparable letters in the form of a liquid or thread which dangled from his mouth, long and silky, endless and unbroken, and which became entangled and intertwined like a cocoon. One letter might perhaps be able to separate of its own accord and fly through the air as a droplet of water or a bubble which would presently fall onto some solid object.

She was paying attention to him. He was no ordinary guest. He had been a friend of her husband's for many a long year, more years than she and her husband had been together, longer than her husband had known anyone. He was a well-bred man. She could tell by his tense facial muscles and the way his neck was contracted and his necktie tightly knotted, as though it were never, could never be undone, as though he slept and awoke with it on, even as though he were born with it on. And that jacket with its two rows of buttons and the tight trousers carefully buttoned and the legs clenched and knees tight, sitting like a bashful woman or a virgin girl. Yes, he had the virginal look of a man who seems never to take off his clothes, or whose clothes *could* never come off, even if he wanted.

His presence in the house, even in her husband's absence, did not disturb her in the slightest. She let him talk in his chair while she did what she wanted, perhaps write, perhaps read. If her pen fell and rolled under the table, she could bend over to pick it up without embarrassment. If her short, tight skirt rode up to uncover her from behind, she was not upset. He could not possibly look at her. And if he did look, his expression was refined, cultured, resting as lightly and dispassionately on her body as air. Even his incessant talking did not disturb her in the slightest, but was perhaps entertaining, since when he was not there, she would put the radio on.

He turned his back to the mirror and remained standing. She was sitting in front of him in an armchair, her thighs half naked and half open, the natural position of the thighs of a modern woman when she is sitting. His eyes could easily penetrate between them and reach the top with no trouble at all. He had gone from talking about international politics to the origin of existence to fatalism in religion. But, as he talked, his neck muscles tensed up and suddenly emitted a strange squeak which he feared was audible, so that he had to raise his voice louder than modern etiquette demanded. He felt somewhat embarrassed, but as his voice rang out in the salon with its modern furniture and gently fluttered the diaphanous curtain hanging at the windows so that it tickled his ear, he suddenly loved the sound of his voice and the pronunciation of words filled him with great delight.

The book was still in her hands, her eyes on a line at the top of a page. She did not move her eyes from word to word. She really loved books, but her dislike of reading was even greater. Despite herself, her glance slipped from the sentence onto her long silvered nails manicured like talons. As the softness of the expensive paper flowed into her fingertips, she felt a tangible link between herself and culture.

He remained standing, his back to the mirror. She had not yet looked up from the book. All that happened, when his voice suddenly broke off, was that she reached out automatically to the radio so that the room was filled with a sedate voice reciting the Qur'an. Perhaps if it had been another programme, not one quite so decorous, such as a play or a piece of music, he might have moved from his place. But as it was the recitation of the Qur'an and in so dignified a voice, he could do nothing other than remain standing, immobile, where he was. It was winter time – the last day of January to be exact – and despite the sturdy, firmly-fixed windows, a draught of cold air blew onto his spine. He considered reaching out to pick up an article of clothing lying at his feet, but he feared that, were he to move, he would attract her attention before the recitation had finished. He was only able to gaze sorrowfully at his expensive English wool sweater spreading its warmth over the floor tiles. Beside it was his tie with its tight and respectable knot and long, narrow, shiny tail; and next to it, almost attached to it, were his large coarse cotton underpants revealing the size of his stomach and the shape of his thighs, exposing them without compassion or modesty and without regard for accepted manners.

The recitation ended. He started to think of what movement he could begin with. He imagined that moving the arms might be more appropriate than anything else. And perhaps he actually did move his arms because the thick hair beneath his armpits became visible. But not the slightest trace of embarassment showed in her. She was still sitting reading her book, her thighs half naked, half open, the natural position of the thighs of a modern woman absorbed in reading, the natural absorption of a cultured person. He would not have thought, it would never have occurred to him, that absorption in anything, no matter how deep or cultural, could come between a woman and a naked man.

Picking up the voice of the reciter, she automatically reached out and somewhat fearfully turned the dial. A thunderous voice began broadcasting the news. Had she been alone, she might have turned the dial again, but she knew that he was sitting in his chair, his neck tense and knotted with a tie, his upper half carefully encased by two rows of buttons, his thighs pressed tightly together in modesty, the natural position of the thighs of a modern man listening to a broadcast. Her eyes had wandered from the sentence to peek furtively at her smooth white arms and, finding a few coarse obtrusive hairs, she remembered her appointment with the beautician.

He was beginning to feel confused. What should he do to draw her out of her absorption? Put his fingers in his mouth and whistle as he used to as a child playing barefoot and half naked in the street? Perhaps he really did put his fingers in his mouth, but he did not whistle. The muscles of his mouth were no longer capable of producing such vulgar sounds. He remained standing as stiff and naked as a statue. Suddenly, silence fell on the room. Perhaps there had been a power-cut. As she raised her head from the book, the room was suddenly plunged into darkness. She would have stumbled into him as she made her way towards the library had he not taken a step backwards. When she returned with another book, the electricity had returned and he was sitting in his usual chair in full possession of his clothes and his dignity.

The Square

The Square

He was lying in that space defined for him in centimetres, beneath him solid smooth ground which exuded cold and damp like bathroom tiles, around him on all sides piles of flesh, soft and hot and sticky, of various shapes and sizes: arms, legs, heads, backs, stomachs . . . all human, judging by the degree of warmth and by the smell of their breath. They may not *all* have been human. He himself could not tell. He had never lain beside a horse or donkey so could not tell the difference, but he was almost certain that they were all human. He was almost certain too that he was one of them, that he was human like them. But he was not absolutely certain. Here things do not appear as they really are, but different, completely different, so different that they are not the same but at times even the absolute opposite. That certainty, for example, was no longer the certainty he was used to, but was very far from certainty and had become more like doubt. And this doubt too was unlike doubt, but was a strange doubt which wavered between doubt and certainty and was neither doubt nor certainty . . . that unusual state which we experience at times, perhaps during sleep; or not exactly sleep but in that fleeting moment prior to sleep or to losing consciousness or perhaps prior to death. It is a moment which I cannot describe, which nobody can describe except someone who has experienced death, who has then revived and taken up a pen to describe that moment to us in detail. And that has never happened.

But, for him, the matter is not that important. None of the things that concern us concern him. Even thinking in this way, about whether what is happening to him is certain or uncertain, whether he is lying down or not, whether this moment he is experiencing within the bounds of time is in wakefulness or sleep or death. These are all minor details which do not concern him, for he is concerned with something far more important, engrossed in something essential to him now, absolutely essential and obligatory . . . a necessity which does not cross our minds for it is not essential to us; or if it is essential, it is present and available in every place and time . . . like the air we inhale from the atmosphere without it being exhausted, like the earth on which we walk and run without it collapsing under our weight or being cramped by our size.

But he is not one of us. Or, to be more exact, he is no longer one of us. Many things have changed for him. It was not a gradual, slow change like that which happens in normal human life, but a sudden change . . . like a storm which rages and sweeps over everything, or a flood which drowns everything, or an earthquake or volcano which destroys everything. Thus, in one minute, everything is changed, in one of those moments which precede the first appearance of the threads of day, which precede the first appearance of the threads of consciousness . . . before one is completely awake from sleep and before one puts on a suit and shoes. Yes, there was no time to put on a suit and shoes, but he was determined to do so. How can he leave his house without a suit and shoes? A few seconds were lost putting them on and now there was no time to say goodbye to his young son asleep in the next room. He wished he'd said goodbye before leaving, but this did not seem necessary at that moment. Wearing a suit and shoes did seem more necessary. Yes, some things seemed more necessary than others. Dinner parties with the head of department seemed more necessary than spending an evening with his young son. Everything to do with the head of department seemed more necessary than any other thing. But he had taken off his suit, taken off his shoes, no longer used them; and his young son would awaken to find that he had disappeared without telling him.

But none of this occurs to him now. Thinking about his son is no longer necessary. Thinking about others is a luxury. And what a luxury it was to think of a person other than himself, to think of a thing other than his body, this body of his which he had not imagined to be of such a size and vastness. He had never previously known the size of his body. He had perhaps known its height and weight, but the size? Which of us so much as thinks about knowing the size of our bodies, of assessing the space that they occupy? None of us thinks about this and it is never necessary to do so since the

81

distance between the earth and the sky is wide enough for all people, not only wide enough but abundantly wide.

But the matter is no longer as it was. Everything has changed with frightening rapidity. There is no longer a sky, but a high wall out of which protrude long thin spokes like metal bars. And the earth is no longer the earth but small squares drawn and defined like a page in a graph book. He possesses one square only, which, if measured with a ruler, would not increase or decrease one centimetre. But it may decrease if the number multiplies; and the number may multiply, always does multiply, like a living cell continually dividing and multiplying.

But now he is not thinking of what will be later, whether the number will increase or not, whether the space defined for him will decrease or not. This matter does not concern him, for thoughts of the future are a luxury which only one who in his thoughts transcends and overcomes the present moment can enjoy. But he is living in the present moment, or, more exactly, it lives him and contains him. He lives within it and it surrounds him with a web like a spider. This, in itself, is something strange and frightening, for instead of him living the moment and taking it over, it suddenly grasps him, winds itself around him and takes him over.

But he is not taken over at all. He does not disappear, even if he wants to. He remains, exists, despite everything. Indeed, his existence is the only thing of which he is aware and his body is the only thing he feels. He has never before been so aware of his existence or felt his body so much. The body as such, or as a certain lump of flesh, has a weight and size which we do not feel. We carry it with us everywhere without hesitation and without encumbrance. When we eat, it eats without impediment; when we have sex it has sex with us without embarrassment; when we sleep it sleeps.

But for him, things have become different. He doesn't know how they became different, nor why. He knows nothing. All he knows is that he was one of the people, had a wife and son and house and a bed to sleep on. He had an office with a messenger at the door and he had a boss who was head of department. He worked hard . . . all the day and into the night. He did not know exactly what he worked at, but he worked with utter confidence and received an adequate wage for his work. His reputation was good; he carried out his religious obligations, did not drink or gamble or steal or lie. Actually, he did perhaps lie sometimes, the sort of lie which isn't really a lie. He used to accompany the head of department to a supper party and tell his wife that he was going to a meeting of the standing committee. That sort of white lie which angered no one except his wife. And his wife's anger was nothing worth mentioning, since it did him no harm worth mentioning.

So he had been one of the people: normal, respectable, with a good reputation, a house with three rooms, a bed on which to sleep and stretch out his legs without hindrance. So what had happened? When? And how? And why? Was it some sort of punishment? And if it was a punishment, what had he done to deserve it? And who had ordered and ratified it?

Many questions which occur to us do not occur to him now. For questions relate to things past and thoughts of the past, like thoughts of the future, are a luxury which only one who transcends or is capable of transcending the present can enjoy. But he is unable to escape the grasp of the present moment. He has fallen into it and it encompasses him and restrains him and he can do nothing other than revolve within it for ever or be choked and die and disappear.

But he does not disappear at all. Nothing indicates such a disappearance. His body is still his body and seems even larger than he thought. He had never thought his body was so large, that his legs, when he stretched them, could become so long. If only he were smaller; if only his legs were shorter . . . perhaps he would have been able to curl up more easily . . . perhaps he would have been able to occupy his defined space better . . . that small square of earth . . . drawn and defined with a ruler, never increasing by one centimetre, however large his body grew, however long his legs, however high his rank, however good his relations with the head of department. Everyone here is equal: the thin and the fat, the tall and the short, the educated and the uneducated, the messenger and the director, all are equal . . . as equal as the teeth of a comb, dressed in the same material, eating from the same plate, urinating into the same receptacle, lying on small tile-like squares, drawn and defined and equal, each with one square only.

This equality in itself is something awesome and frightening. It is not equality in the sense that everyone eats from the same plate or wears the same material or urinates with everybody else into one receptacle or lies with everyone else in one square. It is not an equality which actually happens but rather a *feeling* of equality, the feeling of being one of this mound of flesh piled up in adjacent rows. Nothing distinguishes him from it, nothing proves that he is himself and not someone else. No name, no title, no clothes, no certificate, no rank, no badge, not even a signature or fingerprint. He does not hate equality, or, to be more exact, had not hated equality. He had read a lot about it and had been excited by it. Often he had been moved by the sight of a child begging or been angered at the sight of a well-fed wealthy man. He was often moved and often angered and each time, he was genuine . . . more genuine than at any previous time, so genuine that at times the tears had gushed from his eyes. But now he no longer remembers anything, for memory is a luxury which only one who can lie on his back or stomach and stretch out his legs without hindrance can enjoy. But he cannot stretch his legs, for the space is small, no more than one tiled square and around him are arms and legs and heads and stomachs, surrounding him on all sides, pressing on him from all directions as he tries, with all his strength and with all his effort, to curl himself up, to shrink, to contract, to diminish, to squeeze himself into the defined space and enter the square. He does not know how that can happen, how his vast body can shrink to such a small size, how he can curl himself up into the size of a foetus. How this can happen he does not know. But he does know that it has to happen. There is no other solution. The space is defined and the square only one, and there is no reason for it to increase one centimetre. His body is still his body with its density and size undiminished and under no circumstances can he return to being a foetus. But he must enter the square. Yes, he must. Why must he? And how? He does not know, but he knows that it must happen. Perhaps after enormous, superhuman effort, perhaps after an infinite time, perhaps after anything, but in the end it will happen.

But it is not happening. His body retains its size. Around him are hot and sticky arms, legs, heads and stomachs, surrounding him on all sides, pressing and pressing. But he is not pressed; neither does his shape and size change, like a drop of mercury resisting any pressure and under any weight remaining a drop of mercury. And he is no weaker than a drop of mercury. He resists with all his strength, resists the size of his body and the length of his legs, resists the density of his flesh and bones, resists with all his strength, with all his force and thoughts. He resists without ceasing, without slacking or despairing. He curls himself up and shrinks and withdraws into himself like a snake trying to squeeze into a narrow hole, exactly like a snake . . . not exactly, for he is not a snake but a person, more flexible, more forceful, more capable. He had an office and a messenger boy and a head of department. He had a wife and son and house with three rooms. He had a bed . . . yes, he had a large bed, on which he stretched out his legs and lay on his back or stomach and closed his eyes and dreamed. He dreamed like anyone else, willingly or unwillingly. He dreamed of supper parties with the head of department, of exceptional promotion, of equality amongst people. Yes, he used to dream every night, like anyone else. Perhaps he is dreaming now. But the bed is not beneath him, only the ground as hard and damp as the bathroom floor and his eyes are not shut, his legs not stretched out horizontally as in sleep, but doubled up over his stomach and under his back. How can his legs bend so far? How have his joints become so supple? How do his bones bend? He does not know. He was no yoga expert, but a thinking man living by his intelligence who did not move a muscle except when absolutely necessary. From lack of movement, his joints had dried and hardened. They creaked sometimes when he sat down or stood up, like rusty door hinges, although that didn't matter to him, for after all, he was still able to walk and sit and stand and eat and have sex. Besides, it was not only *his* joints which creaked. He often heard his colleagues' joints, even those of the head of department.

But all this has changed in an astonishing way. Nobody would imagine that this round, curled-up mound was originally a man or could ever be a man after being loosened and extended. No one would imagine. But it is not a matter of imagining or dreaming. It is real; as real as the ground hard and cold under his buttocks; as real as the warmth with a human smell which fills his nose; as real as the existence of his body with its weight and size . . . an existence more real than any other thing so that nothing other seems to be real; nothing other seems to exist or to have ever existed. Not his office or messenger boy or head of department or wife or son or house or even his bed. Perhaps all his former life was a dream . . . a very long dream. Perhaps it was hope or illusion or supplication. Now he is in that small defined space with his huge body, trying to enter the square. But he does not enter. The square is smaller than his body, his body larger than the square. But he must enter, this moment must pass. This moment which contains him, encompasses him and restricts him like a bridle or a metal chain . . . this vast and growing moment, stretching into eternity. How can one moment of time be so long? How had moments passed before? Can this moment pass . . .? He does not know. But he knows that it must pass. Perhaps after a very long time. How long he does not know. Perhaps after enormous, superhuman effort. But in the end it will pass . . . it will pass just like any other moment in life . . . and perhaps with the very same ease . . .

Man

Man

In one rare moment – so rare that few people (perhaps only a very few people) experience it – luck was with her. Or in other words, it betrayed her. For, suddenly and inexplicably, she found herself face to face with life, stark and real, like a bolt striking someone dead in an instant, the secret dying with them. Or they may be more resilient and do not die completely, but enter a state somewhere between consciousness and unconsciousness, so confused that they can neither distinguish reality from unreality nor wakefulness from sleep.

At one such moment, Khadija stretched out her hand and opened the door. As though struck by an electric current, she lost her power of movement and speech. Her body was rooted to the spot and the blood froze in her veins. Her heart would have stopped beating and life would have left her totally had her eyes not retained their power of sight, as though life had retreated from her body to concentrate in them. Khadija could see the strange scene. Although she could not really tell whether it was a dream or reality, she could see him clearly. At the first glimpse of Ashmawi's head, she recognized his curly hair and the thick nape of his dark neck. But at that moment, it seemed to her like the head of a strange man, not one she had ever seen before nor lived with for ten whole years. Perhaps it was this that made her contemplate the sight without feeling, as indifferently as one watches the scenes of a film or play; or as if it were a circus in which animals perform amazing feats that are so surprising that one exclaims: my goodness!

When Khadija's mouth opened and her amazed and hoarse voice exclaimed: my goodness! two pairs of wide, dismayed eyes immediately met her own staring ones. She was so terrified that the four eyes seemed inhuman to her; but she quickly recognized those of Ashmawi by the yellowish whites and hooded lids. The other eyes vanished the moment they appeared as though they were only a single frame in a film and not the real eyes of a living embodied person.

At first glance, Ashmawi too was confused and not completely certain that those staring eyes looking at him were the sunken and angry eyes of Khadija. Perhaps he too could not tell whether what was happening was real or only a nightmare. Unconsciously, he put out a hand to feel his body to make sure he was awake and his fingers came upon his naked back. Reality struck him like a heavy wall under which he could not move. All he could do was bury his face in the thick Persian carpet, but the rest of his body remained where it was, on the ground, visible, naked and exposed. Khadija saw him clearly, could count every one of his vertebrae. She had not thought his body so thin, his shoulder blades so small and sharp. In his suit, he appeared to her full and broad-shouldered. The first time he'd come to ask her father for her hand, she'd agreed instantly. His father was a tenant farmer on their land; but he had educated his son in school. Ashmawi became a government employee wearing a suit. She had often rejected suitors from the village, even the *Omda*'s[1] son who alone owned ten *feddan*[2] of land but who was not employed by the government and who still wore *galabias*. True, they were made of expensive cotton, but they were still *galabias* which hung off his shoulders and swung around his legs like a woman's. For a man to be a man, he must have shoulders which do not droop but are straight and broad, which is just what a jacket does for him. And he must have legs, each separate from the other so he could move each on its own confidently and freely. That, for her, was the characteristic which distinguished masculinity from femininity and which could only occur because of trousers.

For the first time in her life Khadija saw Ashmawi without clothes. She had seen him in pyjamas before he went to bed and when he got up, but she had never seen him completely undressed. Even in those moments when she could have seen him without clothes on, she did not dare open her eyes. She was a virtuous woman, from a good family, and it was not right for her to look at such times. It was not virtue alone which stopped her, but also the fear and utter dread of spying on so grave a thing as a man's body. She dreaded him and shunned him. Whenever he approached her and put his arms around her, she shuddered. She could not picture any wife being happier than she, nor a husband more loving than Ashmawi. Yes, Ashmawi loved her, that was for sure. He made every effort to make her happy . . . every effort.

The words 'every effort' formed themselves into a lump in her throat. Vague old feelings began to emerge from some obscure recess deep within her, like a pin boring into her skull to dislodge some strange idea which wouldn't have crossed her mind. Ashmawi made every effort to please her. Pleasing her was hard for him. He tried to please her against his will, against his own desire. Ashmawi did not desire her, had never loved her. Even at the height of ecstasy when he showered her with gifts and love, even at the peak of lovemaking, there was always that obscure feeling deep within her separating him from her like a pane of cold glass or like a chronic festering boil which will neither come to the surface and burst nor be devoured by white blood cells and die. But she hadn't felt it, had always been able to ignore it. At times she had scolded herself and had accused her body of inordinate desire and greed. At other times, nothing had helped and the bitterness rose from its deep-seated hidden place so that she could almost taste it gripping her insides.

As if a veil or a cloud lifted from Khadija's memory, she began to remember things she had not remembered before, to notice things she had not noticed before. How many times Ashmawi had gone away on unexpected business. Every night he had gone out on the pretext of having to attend meetings. How many nights she had spent lying awake, tossing and turning, while he slept beside her snoring. When he approached her, after all her attempts to be open, and tried to please her, most of

94

the time it had not worked. Perhaps he had never pleased her. She had fooled him and fooled herself. But her body often betrayed her and had kept clinging to him, pleading and dying for the end to come. But it did not come; neither did her body stop wanting. It remained tense and unyielding and nothing could free it other than exhaustion and fatigue so that it fell, quivering and trembling like a slaughtered chicken, then presently quietened completely and stopped moving.

Ashmawi had still not moved from his place. Khadija saw and knew. Why should he make any effort? He often made an effort, often tried to make an effort. But now she knew. She had come to him of her own accord so she had to bear the consequences. She was a woman, no matter what, and he was still the man. Maybe she hadn't quite seen him as a man, but for her he was a man. And not just any man, but a respectable employee and the director of the chief attorney's office. Whenever she went to his office, at any time of the day, she saw with her own eyes how the other employees, great or small, bowed to him; how general directors asked his permission to see the chief attorney; how he could ask for any one of them on the telephone. When Ashmawi had graduated from the teachers' training college, he had had two posts to chose from: either to be a teacher or to be private secretary to a director. He had refused to be a teacher. What was it worth? One lived as a teacher and died as a teacher, or at most as a headmaster. But to be the private secretary of a director, to attach oneself to an important person as lice attach themselves to the scalp, meant that the way was open. All those employees who had arrived before him had a firm attachment to an important person. Was there any connection firmer than being a private secretary?

Ashmawi was one of those people who are made for being a private secretary, the type who have no private personality or private thoughts or private opinion or private life, nor even a private body, but who are a jelly-like lump as transparent as a pane of glass through which another personality can be seen, like a mirror reflecting an image, always the image of another, an image superimposed on the original but never the original itself.

Ashmawi did not know what the work of private secretary entailed exactly, but he believed that he had to play the role of bodyguard, to turn his body into a plate of armour for his director, or later for the chief attorney, to put his body between him and the people, to hang around him at every meeting, to turn his office into a sort of sieve with holes which held back all except certain persons of a certain size and weight. A private secretary was trained to recognize their accents on the telephone, their walk as they entered his office, the way they put cigarettes into their mouths and removed them from the corner, the way they talked, particularly when referring to the attorney, for example, as 'Majid *Bek'*, whether the way they pronounced the word '*Bek'* was as inferior to a superior or as equal to equal or as one *Bek* to another. Sometimes they did not say 'Majid *Bek'* but 'Professor Majid'; for some of them it was enough to say simply 'Majid' for the private secretary to understand the level of intimacy between them and the chief attorney. All these small things called for attention to detail to which Ashmawi became accustomed and which he mastered to perfection. After some experience, he realized that his work consisted of no more than a collection of rituals that were small, very small but important, very important. There always had to be two office boys in front of the chief attorney's door. Before the chief attorney went out or before he went in, there had to be a tremor in their backs; then the two had to jump to attention simultaneously, their arms raised at the same moment, forefingers to foreheads. Before the chief attorney announced his departure, the limousine had to be half-way up the steps, the chauffeur at the ready, standing to open the back door with his left hand, his right hand ready to be raised the moment the chief attorney's bald head came into view on the first step.

When the chief attorney was settled in his office, there were other minute details which Ashmawi had come to master. He had learned to understand the meaning of any movement of any of the chief attorney's limbs without a need for words. A shake of his head, for example, he had grown to understand immediately. A shake of the head was not always a simple shake of the head. There was a shake which meant that the chief attorney was satisfied; there was a shake which meant that he was dissatisfied. There was a shake of the head which meant that Ashmawi had to remain where he was and place himself fully and squarely in front of a visitor; and a shake which meant that Ashmawi had to leave.

Ashmawi became expert. When he was transferred from the director's office to the director general's office and from there to the chief attorney's, he had no need of new expertise, for the manner was the same manner everywhere, the domain of the private secretary was the same domain, the employees' customs the same customs, the relationship of superior to inferior the same, the personality of employee the same personality. He was soft-spoken before his boss and roared like a lion before his inferiors. Every employee, according to his rank, had a particular way of pronouncing the word *Bek*, a particular way of holding a file. Ashmawi had learned to recognize the rank of an employee from his bearing, voice and movements.

Ashmawi had also realized that there was something more important than expertise: obeying orders, whether personal or general. One of the directors used to send him every morning to take his child to school. Another used to leave his 'lady' in his care to take shopping. Another director would send him to the market to buy the week's meat. Yet another director urged him to learn chess so that he could play with him in his free time. As for the chief attorney, he had another curious hobby.

The chief attorney was one of those men who believe they are more virile than any other man. He was possibly not quite so sure of that, but he always wanted to prove it. He did not know exactly what to do to achieve it, but he always felt, whenever another man appeared before him, a violent desire to subjugate him. Subjugation for him did not mean that ordinary type of subjugation which can take place between a superior and an inferior, but it was rather a brutish desire to annihilate him intellectually, mentally, even physically, so that nothing of him remained.

He had many ways of subjugating: sometimes softly, sometimes forcefully, sometimes gently, sometimes by withdrawing. Sometimes he would give and be so full of giving that a person would derive pleasure from tasting the easy life and his buttocks would get used to riding in an upholstered car every day from home to the office and from the office to home; his wife would get used to the new apartment and the new budget whilst he adapted to refined relations and the exercise of authority. And then suddenly he would drop him where he'd found him . . . to his original salary, without suits, without attending meetings, to being jammed into a bus like a sardine, to signing the attendance sheet and leaving to the minute, to being in an office shared with four others without a telephone and without an office boy at the door.

Ashmawi had experienced all this and had learned how to benefit all along the line in return for small, imperceptible concessions, concessions of an invisible or abstract kind which go by the name of respect or masculinity or esteem, or other such intangible qualities. He had realized for sure that such qualities were not abstract. He had never seen a poor man without authority enjoy any of these qualities; neither did he feel, when he conceded something, that he lost anything of the kind. If he did, in his heart of hearts, feel that he had lost something, it was always something extremely small in his view, amounting to no more than a vague invisible feeling. Since his concessions increased day by day and his benefits increased at the same rate, he did not think that a day would finally come when his concessions would increase to such an extent that they would be larger than he could ever have imagined.

Ashmawi never imagined that what happened to him could happen. Before it did happen, he did not imagine that he was conceding anything big, as long as it happened in secret and no one knew about it.

It would have been possible, before his eyes met those of Khadija, for the incident to pass by and vanish as others had done. But the moment his eyes met Khadija's, it was as though a veil fell, as though he woke up to himself and began to feel the fateful consequence of what had happened. He did not realize that he had not only conceded something big, but that it was the largest thing in himself and that his whole being had been crushed. It was not the weight of one thing that crushed him. It was not the weight of the chief attorney alone, but that of all the directors and heads with whom he worked, the weight of all their fat bodies and importance, all their large offices and Persian carpets, their big black and coloured telephones, their long black cars, their red lights, their doors covered with green baize, the red carpets on white marble stairs, the high solid walls hung with pictures in thick golden frames, the mirrors, candles, heaters and smoke-filled halls, ashtrays, chandeliers, dossiers, schedules, grades, units, secret reports, suits and rewards. All of them together accumulated into one weight which pressed on him and weighed on his meagre existence and crushed him and flattened him like a sheet of metal or a cigarette paper.

Khadija was still staring at Ashmawi who had not moved, hiding his face in the Persian carpet, his slim body stretched out alongside the huge desk which reached half-way up the wall, on top of which was a pane of glass with green baize under it, above it a long wooden plaque on which was engraved: *'We made some of you of higher rank than others'*, and behind the desk, a large leather armchair.

Perhaps Khadija was not, until this moment, fully aware of her presence or of the reality of what had happened, but she came round to a strange noise: a suppressed sobbing which grew louder and louder, becoming like a woman's lamentation. Ashmawi was wailing. Khadija did not know what happened to her. It was as though she forgot all she had seen, as though the previous moments had never been, as though she had been asleep, had had a nightmare and had awoken. She found herself kneeling beside Ashmawi, stroking his face and with the palm of her hand wiping away his tears, the tears of Ashmawi, her husband, her man. Whatever happened, he was her man and his tears cut into her like a knife. Whatever happened, he was Ashmawi, the only one she had in this life. Ten years under the same roof, ten bitter-sweet years. And the sweet was so much greater than the bitter. Get up, Ashmawi. With her own two hands, she began to gather up his scattered clothes. With her own two hands, she dressed him in the suit, the suit for which she had chosen him over all the men of the village.

[1] *Omda*: chief of a village
[2] *feddan*: square measure of land

The Man
with Buttons

The Man
with Buttons

About ten years ago, I had a clinic in Benha and had started publishing my writings. A story of mine, entitled 'Husband, I don't love you', appeared in a magazine. A few days later, a young married woman came to me with my story, her lips pursed in disapproval. Then she left me a story she had written. It stayed in the drawer of my desk until I came across it recently, folded up like an old letter.

My dear husband Amin Fadel Afifi.

Some people may be surprised that a wife addresses her husband by his three names. I don't think that anyone in this day and age still calls another by three names, other than security personnel, policemen, officers of court and doctors in the registration office for issuing death certificates.

I make no secret of the fact that I did not know your

three names until five years after we got married, when that policeman came and shouted 'Amin Fadel Afifi' from behind the spyhole in the door. You told me that day that it was to do with an old case which your sister Fahima had brought against you for seizing the ten measures of land which were her inherited share.

Until that day, I had been the obedient wife of a man named Amin *Bek* Afifi. I did not know you very well, for I had never looked directly at your face. But I could tell you from other men by your broad shiny bald head with a black mole in the middle which, our neighbour told me, was a mark of piety and goodness. At that time, I asked her what the connection was between a piece of black skin on the forehead and piety and goodness. She said: It comes from the smooth forehead repeatedly rubbing against the rough ground during regular prayer and long prostration in humility. The fact is that this mole used to hit my eye whenever I looked at you, and worse still, it used to hit my forehead whenever that thing happened between us. Despite the complete darkness in which our bedroom was immersed and which didn't allow me to see anything of you, that mole was always visible, perhaps because it was jet black or because it was so prominent. And despite that distance which always separated our faces — for it never happened that I touched any part of your face or that your lips accidentally touched any part of mine — yet of all the parts of your body, only that mole was able to bridge the distance between our faces and hit my forehead like a ball of rubber.

When the policemen said 'Amin Fadel Afifi' to you, the colour of your face changed. I was surprised that day at how your three names could seem like a curse. Later, after the man had gone, you told me that the police were 'louts', from the countryside, and did not know how to address people. I did not ask you what 'louts' meant, but I'd heard you use the word before and did not understand it. The first time I heard it from you, the colour of your face changed. And when the colour of your face changes, I know you are angry or frightened. With a bit of practice, I have become able to tell the difference between the colour of anger and the colour of fear. When a bus ran into us, your face turned white tinged with yellow. That's the colour of fear. And when you are angry and beat the servant with your old shoes, the white also becomes tinged with yellow, a different yellow. But the real colour of your face, I don't know.

You used to say 'lout' in a rough voice thick with saliva so that the word itself took on a tangible thickness which made it strike my ear, just as the mole used to strike my forehead. From the conversation between you and your friend in the sitting room, I gathered that this 'lout' was the new boy who had been appointed two days earlier as a junior in your office and who called you 'Amin Afifi' instead of 'Amin *Bek* Afifi'. Your friend was busy cleaning his ear with a matchstick, but, after taking it out and studying the end of it, said that some university lads did not know how to address their superiors, that education had failed miserably, that universities no longer taught anything.

I used to sit in the hall and listen in to your conversation with your friend every night as the two of you sat in the sitting room. I would make tea which the servant took in in small glasses, once, twice, three times, ten times. The two of you talked about nothing other than that new boy. The descriptions of him pro-liferated: once as a lout, once as empty-headed, once as an imbecile. The description 'mad' was bestowed on him after he had whispered to one of his young col-leagues that he did not believe in the 'Everlasting' and another of his colleagues transmitted this whisper to you word for word.

I did not know what the word 'Everlasting' meant exactly and thought it was the name of your boss in the office, but I understood from the conversation between you and your friend that the 'Everlasting' is one of the names of Almighty God.

After your friend leaves, you turn off the light in the sitting room and see me sitting in the hall, staring into the darkness. You go to bed, stretching out your body as long and huge as a crocodile and there is barely enough room left for me. So I sleep on the couch, except for that night every month or two months or three when you suddenly, and for no reason that I know of, remember that I am there on the couch and you call to me with a rough voice thick with saliva and I know that that thing will happen and that the black mole will strike my forehead, that my body will become as sluggish as a stagnant pool, with nothing in the heart, neither pain nor joy, and the skin growing cold and deathly still. I used to be surprised at my legs, at how heavy they were as I walked from the hall to the bedroom. My whole body grew heavy, like a sick or aged person whose joints have grown stiff, whereas my legs are light when I go up to our neighbour and I climb six flights of steps without feeling my legs or body and without panting.

Our neighbour was not alone in the house. There was another person sitting in a dark corner whom I couldn't see. I told myself that it was probably a woman. But he turned his head towards me and at that moment and for the first time in my life, I discovered the difference between a man and woman. A charge, like a throb, leapt in one split second and in one bound from my heart to my mouth, as hot as blood. It hurt a bit, somewhere under my ribs, on the left side, there in one specific round point exactly above the lower half of the heart. It was not pain, but it became painful for a second and exciting to the point of fear, with a happiness as sharp as a needle piercing the flesh which ran in a shiver across the skin like fever convulsing the body.

Our neighbour told him in a subdued voice that I was the wife of Amin *Bek* Afifi. He smiled without moving and said: Amin Afifi the clerk. For the first time, I learned you had another third name. It too seemed like a curse, but I was not as taken aback as on the day the police came. But I felt so ashamed that drops of sweat began to gather on my forehead. Each drop had its own form whose weight and roundness I could feel, one next to the other, as if suddenly a number of moles, just like yours, were growing on my forehead.

I tried to defend you. Fifteen years under one roof, three meals each day, I used to see you sneak a glance at my plate to count the bread rolls before I ate. But I defended you and said you were not Amin Afifi the clerk. And worse than that, he added other descriptions which I did not know and told stories about you which I had not heard. He even told the story of your sister Fahima and the policeman and the ten measures which you stole from her. And he laughed as he described you when you went to see your boss once, having done up only three buttons of your jacket. It seems that when

109

you heard the bell, you buttoned up the fourth in a hurry so that it did not go into the buttonhole, or only a small part of it went in. Anyway, as soon as you appeared before your boss, this fourth button came out of its hole.

As he was telling me the story, I remembered your conversation with your friend about this incident. I heard the word 'buttons' repeated many times, but I was sleepy that night and did not pay much attention to the conversation. It seemed to me to be a minor matter and not so serious that you had to write to your boss to apoligize.

Our neighbour reminded me it was time to go down to you, but I was feeling very ashamed and remained standing, hesitant. In fact, at that exact moment, a faint light fell on his face and chest and it seemed to me that he was inviting me to him with a slow signal of his hand.

This time we touched each other. For the first time, I discovered the touch and softness of my body. When my hand touched my skin, I felt a movement like electricity in my fingers, I fell in love with my arms and legs and I almost hugged myself. My body got lighter and lighter. When I walked, the tips of my toes hardly touched the ground for I was on a cushion of air which separated my feet from the earth. Walking seemed to me like swimming in water, water lighter than sweet water.

I said to him: What's your name?

He said: What does a name matter!

I said: What do you do?

He said: I think and sit in a dark corner and don't leave it.

I said: Don't you have a boss or people under you?

He said: I don't have buttons to do up. None of my clothes have buttons.

I said: I will stay with you. You are the only man I have met.

He said: But you're not the first women I have met.

I said: So be it. I don't mind.

He said: But I do mind.

I said: Why?

He said: I don't have enough time.

I said: Why did you introduce yourself to me?

He said: To save you from death.

I said: You leave me to return to death.

He said: You will not return as you were. You will be reborn and will return a new woman.

I said: I will not accept my life as I did before.

He said: That's how it should be.

I said: I will go mad.

He said: That's how it should be.

I said: Are you telling me to go mad?

He said: Yes, that's the way to salvation.

I laughed hysterically as I said goodbye to him and made for the stairs to go down the six flights. When I saw you coming in the door, I don't know how, but my hands reached out, rained blows and punches on you and pulled off all your buttons.

Your wife, Firdous

Them

Them

His narrow sunken eyes do not show what is happening inside him for they are covered by a thin darkish membrane. He does not know if, together with bony fingers, a fat globous nose and a hollow ribcage, he has inherited it from his mother; or whether it creeps in from the corner of his moist eyelids as a whiteish dewy substance which gathers under or above the lid; or whether it comes from a hole concealed somewhere between his nose and eyes or perhaps between his ears and eyes. He does not know. All he knows is that the sticky white substance comes every day and always gathers to rest finally in the corner of his eyes, to consume them as a weevil consumes cotton bolls, making him rub away at them with his fingers as if he wants to pluck them from his face, just as a decaying boll is plucked from the cotton plant.

Hassan was squatting, his knees as bony as the head of a walking stick covered by the hem of his *galabia*. He craned his head to see the *Omda*, the village chief, in his ample *caftan* and large woollen *kuffiya*, sitting on a chair. Around him were other men sitting on chairs, wearing woollen *caftans* and *kuffiyas*. The strong voice of the *Omda* was saying with enthusiasm, as he pointed with his little finger: I speak on behalf of them! From under the darkish membrane, Hassan's eyes were glued to the *Omda*'s finger, following to where it pointed . . . He saw the finger hover in the air, then finally come to rest on them as they sat on the ground, their bony knees covered by the hems of their *galabias*, looking at the *Omda* and his men with half darkened eyes and half opened mouths . . . some were smiling, some were scowling, some were overcome by fatigue and their lips drooped unawares . . .

A cold breeze blew and Hassan clenched his lips as he gazed at the *Omda*'s moist pink lips and began licking his own with his sparse saliva. He heard the *Omda* say once again: I speak on behalf of them! The word 'them' struck Hassan's ear, then resounded like a ball of rubber hitting the ground. He craned his neck to the right and brought his head close to that of his companion, stealing some warmth from his breath, and whispered in his ear: What does 'them' mean? His companion's mouth gaped in surprise seasoned with an aroma of onions and said: Don't you know what it means? It's simple as can be! A few drops of embarrassment fell from Hassan's head onto his sallow face, like drops of dew falling onto the surface of a brackish pool and spreading a slight movement over its stillness . . . He looked at the man in confusion and embarrassment and said: But what does it mean? The man stretched his neck haughtily and said: It means . . . then fell silent for a minute, pursing his lips and closing off the smell of onion. Then he looked at Hassan and said: It means – them there – understand? Hassan hid his head in his collar and withdrew into himself, silent.

But he came round to hear the *Omda* repeat in a loud voice, his lips even pinker and more invigorated: I speak on behalf of them! The word 'them' again struck his ear and again resounded like a rubber ball falling to the ground. He craned his neck to the left, bringing his head close to his other companion and, stealing some warmth from his breath, whispered in his ear: What does 'them' mean? The man looked at him with listless eyes, his lower lip drooping onto his chin, and said: Dunno. Hassan leant forward until he was close to the man sitting in front of him and stealing some warmth from him, whispered: What does 'them' mean? The man's lips parted in a dry grimace and he said: It means the men who wear woollen *caftans* and *kuffiyas*! Look, he's pointing at them!

Hassan raised his head and squinted to focus on the little finger of the *Omda*, following its movement until he saw it finally come to rest on themselves sitting on the ground. Hassan once again brought his mouth near to the ear of his companion in front, again stealing some warm breath, and whispered: His little finger's pointing at us. The man once again pursed his lips in a scowl and said angrily: You're not looking! His index finger's pointing at the men with *caftans*!

Hassan stretched his neck in order to see the *Omda*'s fingers, to count each one and follow the movement of the big and little ones . . . Hassan saw that all the *Omda*'s fingers moved in time to his lips in many different directions: some up, some down, some to the right, some to the left, some to the middle, some a little below the middle, some a little above the middle, some a little to the right of the middle, some a little to the left. Hassan's eyes went to and fro, up and down, with them, until his eyelids began to discharge a whiteish dew into the corner of his eyes to lie there and consume them . . .

Hassan lowered his eyes and rubbed them with his fingers, wanting to pluck them from his face so that the fire burning in them would cease. Once again the booming voice of the *Omda* struck his ears . . . the word 'them' again hit the bones of his head like a solid ball. He looked around in confusion . . . to the right, to the left, to the front. Feeling warm air brush his neck from behind, he turned round and saw a man sitting behind him listening to the *Omda*'s words, his mouth open and breath panting. He leaned back until his head touched the man's and, drawing power from his warm ample breath, put his mouth to his ear and said: What does 'them' mean? The man did not look at him and quickly replied: Listen and keep quiet! Don't meddle in what doesn't concern you!

Hassan took his mouth away from the man's ear, clutched his arms around himself and crouched up inside his *galabia* silently.

Despite himself, his eyes again stole towards the *Omda*'s fingers, determined to see, to find out. But the *Omda*'s fingers were wagging about erratically in all directions. Hassan looked around and saw the four men surrounding him in front, behind, to the right and to the left, separating him from the rest. However much he craned his neck, he could see no more than the mouth of the man in front or behind or to his right or to his left, those four who constricted him and formed four walls beyond which he could not reach.

Hassan fidgeted in his place. Something in his body began to hurt. Something like a needle pricked his skin and opened some of his mud-blocked pores. He used to be relaxed and did not fidget when he sat. He used to let his buttocks rest happily on the ground and remain sitting quietly until he felt a sharp sting in his knees, when he'd get up, yawning, to collect the maggots from the cotton plants. But now he couldn't relax, couldn't let his buttocks rest happily on the ground, for the needle stung his body. Whether it was in his chest or buttocks or in his skull, he didn't know; all he knew was that it was hiding somewhere under his clothes, under his skin. It stung and hurt him and spoiled his relaxation.

Hassan stuck out his legs from under his *galabia* and shook his limbs in an effort to get rid of the needle which pricked him here and there, like a malicious flea. He felt that his arms and legs were extended as far as possible without hitting any one of the four walls. He looked around in surprise and saw that the *Omda* was leaving, around him the men in *caftans*, behind him men in *galabias*. He got up and hurried after them. He managed to catch up with one of the men who was walking with the help of a wooden stick. He approached him and whispered in his ear: What does 'them' mean? The man stopped, leaning on his stick and said angrily: You're asking me? Did I say it? Why don't you ask the one who did? He waved his arm in the air angrily, hit his stick on the ground and ambled off like an exhausted racehorse.

Hassan stood in the street rubbing his eyes. Alright, why not ask the *Omda*? It was he who had said it, so he most certainly understood it . . .

A few drops of enthusiasm fell from his head onto his sallow face, just as dew drops onto the surface of a brackish pool, giving its stillness some life.

Hassan walked to the *Omda*'s residence. As he

approached the large wooden door, a man wearing a *caftan* and *kuffiya*, a rifle slung across his shoulder, came up to him. He saw the head of the rifle pointed at his head, its mouth gaping like that of a hungry puppy or a thirsty viper. Hassan's legs quaked under the weight of his body and he wished he could lower his buttocks to the ground and rest on it. But he turned to the man with the *caftan* and *kuffiya*, trying desperately not to look inside the bottomless black mouth. And although his tongue was stuck to the roof of his mouth, he managed to stutter a few words and tell the man that he wanted to meet the *Omda*. Hassan didn't know why the pupils of the man's eyes widened as he looked at him. He followed the man's glance as it descended to his feet and noticed his thin bony toes covered with a fine layer of black mud. He felt the man approach him, grab him by the corner of his *galabia* and pull him along behind him like a dead rat. Hassan found himself in a wide room. Before him was another man wearing a *caftan* and *kuffiya* carrying a rifle as large as a cannon. Hassan's knees quaked as he averted his glance from its mouth pointed at his head. But the man jabbed the head of the rifle into his shoulder, asking what he wanted. Hassan dislodged his tongue from the roof of his mouth, licked his dry lips, then said: I want to meet the *Omda*. Then he closed his eyes and recited the creed to himself.

Hassan didn't know what happened whilst he was reciting the creed, but when he opened his eyes, he saw the man with the *caftan* and *kuffiya* pointing to another man with a *caftan* and *kuffiya* and, in a daze, felt the large fingers of the man clutch his arm and lead him to a large door. He placed a foot on the threshold, took one small step, then raised his eyes to look in front of him . . . and found himself out in the wide street . . .

Nobody Told Her

Nobody Told Her

The street was long and crowded, the fog thick and dense. Nothing around her was clear, but she did not stop. She was looking for things, things she did not know the name of. But she wanted to know, wanted to be prepared, for something awful was going to happen. Her heart beat wildy, her toes were squeezed into the tips of her pointed shoes, her heels raised on slim posts of wood which clattered loudly and embarrassingly. The shape of her feet was deformed, chafed from beneath and curved from above, just like her mother's, like those of her mother's friends, of all grown women. She hated and feared this resemblance, for grown women were surrounded by strange things which they hid from her in whispers she could not hear, winks she could not understand, low drawn-out laughter and strange things which her mother hid from her in the top drawer of the wardrobe . . . long tied up bundles, layers of thick material . . . and strange looks in her eyes. Particularly in the bath when she helped her wash, her mother's glances became averted and apprehensive, words on the tip of her tongue as if she wanted to disclose something but never did . . . A mysterious danger lurked in her body, with nothing before her except the silent high wall of the bathroom and her mother's rasping breath, over her eyes a cloud which only lifted with the drawn-out laughter and the winks. Even at such times, a thin veil of sadness often remained over her mother's eyes, those of her mother's friends, all grown women; something lay in wait for women, something which frightened her. The clatter of her high heels embarrassed her, her toes squeezed into her shoes hurt her, the curve of her foot sent a tremor through her body, increasing the resemblance between herself and her mother, bringing her closer to that mysterious frightening thing. Her heart did not stop beating; the small bag under her arm and the piastres inside it rattled. But not like the rattle of the tin savings box into which she would drop a piastre or half whenever she longed for some chewing gum. Each day she lifted it up and shook it. The rattle of the piastres sounded sweet to her ears. One day she would open the savings box and be rich and buy a lot of chewing gum and fill her mouth with it, not just a small piece which stuck in her teeth or to the roof of her mouth. The rest she would distribute to her schoolmates at school, all except one of them who chewed gum all day long and never gave her any . . .

Chewing gum was the best thing in her life. The savings box grew heavier. Her body too was no longer light. The stairs which she used to run up three at a time, she no longer ran up, but only took two at a time, and when her feet hit the ground, her body shuddered and she felt a pain, somewhere in her chest, in some place that moved as painfully as the head of a boil. Her trousers no longer fitted; the sides ripped and then they were used as a kitchen rag. She hadn't been given other trousers. She loved riding her bicycle more than anything else, even more than she loved chewing gum, but her mother's eyes, with their averted and apprehensive look, made her hang her head in silence.

Riding a bicycle, too, became fraught with danger; things around her took on a different, uncertain shape. The straight tops of her dresses stuck out in curious folds; her white vests were replaced by coloured shirts with strange straps, just like her mother's. The resemblance scared her, brought her nearer to that fearful thing. Everything that happened in the house was a warning to her. The picture magazines disappeared from their place on the table; the radio which used to play all day was now only for her mother's ears; going out to play in the park became forbidden; even simply walking outdoors and breathing the air was prohibited . . .

Life outside the house was full of mysterious dangers . . . her mother's eyes spied on her body, on every part of it, on every moment, every motion, when she sat in her room, when she slept in her bed, when she went into the bathroom, when she put a hand on her head or stomach. Something was going to happen, something awful, something about which she didn't know, but wanted to know. However awful it was, not knowing was more awful. She wanted to know how to be ready, but her mother did not want to talk and she could not ask. All she could do was search furtively, under the bed, in the wardrobe, in the bathroom, under her clothes, between her fingers and toes, in the folds of her body. Her young heart contracted in fear, her delicate lips clenched in apprehension, her breath gathered in her throat and hardened. Death was the only solution before the catastrophe happened. But death was also frightening. The kitchen knife was blunt and buckled against her stomach and did not enter. Ghosts carrying knives crept about in the darkness, with long fingernails or claws and heads pointed like snakes' fangs. She tried to scream but her voice would not come out; she tried to run but her legs were paralysed. Sleep became a new burden. She did not remember her dreams, but her dreams were unforgettable, for they came in the night and lasted into the day. But her daydreams were not frightening, for she swam in a warm sea, on her body a transparent diaphanous dress, an arm reaching out of the water tickling her, the head of the boil on her chest hurting her. The pain was not strong, but her body trembled, choked by a hidden pleasure. She tried to run, but the arm held her and two eyes looked at her. They were not strange, but resembled those of her father. Her father's eyes made her cry and the arm disappeared behind the tears. But she wanted it. She squeezed her eyelids shut but neither the arm nor her father's eyes came, only other eyes which were like those of the maths teacher.

The story of the maths teacher was a strange one. All the girls at school knew it. One day, the teacher went into the toilet. After she came out, the girls found a cloth covered in red ink . . . A girl whispered in her ear: We don't want a teacher that writes in red ink. Another girl tugged at her clothes, saying that she was frightened of the colour red ever since a large turkey had jumped on

126

her shoulder and bit her when she was wearing a red dress. Another girl came in and whispered in her ear: It's not red ink, you stupid, it's blood . . . a strange disease . . . all maths teachers get it! The rumours spread, winks and words flew about in the air, picked up by small sensitive ears. All teachers . . . no, all girls . . . all women . . . innocent eyes looked around in confusion, small bodies clung together in terror. Not one of them knew the facts. Each one recounted a strange story which she'd heard from her mother or grandmother or adult servant.

Small children are born from women's ears . . . Each of them felt her ear in fear and trepidation. No, not from the ears, from the nose . . . Each put trembling fingers to her nostrils. No, not possible from the nose, the opening's too small, children are not born easily. Something awful happens before that, something mothers don't divulge, a repeated catastrophe . . . every year! Don't be stupid, every month . . . what a disaster!

The waiting was awful, more awful than the catastrophe itself. The disaster would happen to her now. She felt a slight pain inside her . . . no . . . not now . . . not in the street, there were many people around, with thick moustaches and long trousers. It would be a scandal. If only she could curl up and disappear, or the ground open and swallow her up. But the ground did not open. The eyes around her watched her steps, crept up her legs, sized up her buttocks . . . something forbidden in her body, something sinful, shameful. The eyes accused her, the glances surrounded her. She quickened her pace, the thin heels clattering, the piastres under her arm rattling, the secret pain plunging deep inside her. Something awful was going to happen and she wanted to be ready . . . But there were so many shops. The grocery had many bundles, but they were not like her mother's; the stall had many bundles, but they too were not the same. Her toes inside the tips of her shoes were burning, the muscles of her stomach were contracting, her heart was falling and her breathing rose to the sky. The catastrophe was imminent and she was not ready. The things were not there, things whose name she didn't know, whose name nobody knew. She wanted to know but her mother had never told her. Nobody wanted to talk and she could not ask. Her high heels clattered, the piastres under her arm rattled, the long street was crowded, the mist was dense and thick, things around her were hazy, but she walked and did not stop.

The Nose

The Nose

If he was standing on his feet, then why wasn't he as tall as usual? And why weren't all the parts of his body packed together on top of each other in the old arrangement . . . the head on top, under it the neck, then the chest, stomach and legs? And weren't his feet supposed to be planted on the ground . . .?

But apparently this was not so. He was indeed standing; he knew this from the moment he'd arrived at this place. But he was not standing on his feet; rather on something flat and as soft as his stomach. Was he sleeping? But he was wearing a suit, shoes and a tie. The tie was carefully wrapped around his neck, the knot under his chin round and perfectly twisted. Yes, the tie was fixed around his neck. That was a condition of entry into the place.

What was the connection between a long strip of cloth around his neck and respect? After all, there were places more worthy of respect than a neck. And besides, he liked his neck bare, particularly that bulging cartilage, the Adam's Apple, indubitable proof of masculinity. But there are times when one has no need for proof of masculinity or even for masculinity itself. And what the connection was between bulging cartilage in the neck and masculinity, he could not understand.

But things were becoming clearer. They were not things, rather one thing . . . one thing which swallowed all things and became vast . . . vaster than anything he had even seen in his life, vaster than the Great Pyramid itself. When he stood in front of the pyramid, he could raise his head and see its summit. But now he could not see the summit, could not even raise his head . . . his head was not in its usual position where he could move it easily and raise it. It was in a curious horizontal position on the ground, level with his neck, chest, stomach and buttocks, as if he were prostrate, or at least, lying on his stomach.

But he was standing – if standing means being planted on one's feet. He was indeed rooted to the ground by his feet. That was one thing certain, became certain now. The soft flat thing was definitely not his stomach. He pressed on it, pressed with all his weight, until he was almost submerged into it. Perhaps this submersion was the reason for that radical shortening in his height, so that he became a dwarf with his head hardly raised above the ground.

Perhaps it was a trap laid for him. Anything could be a trap these days . . . Although he was cautious and sceptical by nature, at times he made the mistake of being confident. The confidence was not total but hesitant. Things did not seem to be things, words did not seem to be words, he himself did not seem to be himself. He was tall if he stood on his feet, his head raised above his neck, and then he could look upwards.

But his eyes could not see what was above, for the building was vast, vaster than the pyramid, vaster than all the pyramids piled on top of each other in one huge pyramid, its summit higher than the power of sight, its bulk greater than the limits of the five senses. A vast building veiling the sky and the sun behind it, casting its thick black shadow over the ground, over the houses and buildings and streets and cars and government institutions and tram lines.

It was surely a trap. He had to get away. Despite everything, his feet were still capable of moving. Moving the feet was sometimes miraculous. He could raise one foot and lower the other and so move. He did not know where he was escaping to. It was not important to know. He was capable of moving and this ability in itself was an extraordinary thing. He was a dwarf with his head hardly above the ground and the vast building towered in the sky, but he could move whereas the building could not.

The comparison was stupid. Stupidity too was an extraordinary ability. It was not a movement like that of the feet, but was movement inside the head and possibly a physical movement too, but a movement nonetheless and undoubtedly an ability. He searched for his abilities, looking inside his small body for all his hidden weapons. Yes, hidden, for everything had to be done in secret these days, especially when one faced something so vast. It was a building, only a building of stone and incapable of moving, but it was vast. A strange vastness, a vastness which filled the distance between the ground and the sky, a vastness so great it seemed to stretch between the sky and the ground, as though it were a moving thing even though it was as solid an object as the globe, fixed and moving at the same time.

His feet shook. He was cautious and sceptical, but he was no coward. Caution was one thing; cowardice another. He did not recall ever having been afraid of anyone. His feelings for himself were greater than those for others. Simply feelings, or simply delusion. But what was a person? A person was what he deluded himself he was. He deluded himself that he was more capable than others and became more capable than them and his body grew more capable of consuming food . . . every time he sat at the table and felt his stomach swell pleasantly above his thighs, he would tell himself: I'll eat less; and then he'd eat more than ever.

If he ate less, perhaps he'd have been more capable of moving . . . perhaps he would have weighed less . . . perhaps his demands would have been less. But his demands grew day by day. Not only his demands, but those of his wife and children, his acquaintances and friends. There was no one these days who did not have demands and he had many mouths to feed. He had to pay for the delusion that he was more capable than others . . . he had to pay for everything, even for a closed mouth.

He felt his mouth. His lips were there, capable of opening and closing. Yes, that voice coming out was like his own, really was his own, with its familiar timbre and the same words. Even articulating was sometimes miraculous. Articulation in itself was an extraordinary ability. He was a dwarf whose head was hardly raised above the ground, the building was vast and towering, but he was able to articulate whereas the building could not.

That too was an ancient weapon which had stood the test of time. This voice was louder than his own, its timbre more resonant, and it almost deafened him. It may not have been exactly a human voice; the words may not have been articulated the same way he articulated his, but was it necessary for everything to be completely human? Was it necessary for everything to be done in the way he did things? Why did he always judge things by his own body?

His feet shook even more. That stone building was capable of making sounds which were audible in all corners of the sky and earth . . . not just audible but with a voluminous resonance which swallowed up his own voice so that no one heard it. That stone building was also capable of moving. Not a small movement like that of one foot behind the other, but a huge, colossal movement which shook the ground like an earthquake and swallowed up his movements so that no one noticed them. No one heard him, no one noticed him, so what proof was there that he existed? There was no proof.

Sweat poured from his whole body, copious and sticky, with an odour. For the first time in his life, he smelled the odour of his sweat . . . the same odour he so disliked when he came close to others. If he was dead, he would have lost the ability to smell. He existed, therefore. He put his fingers to his nose, to the sole proof that he was not dead. He had never paid much attention to his nose; in his opinion, it was not an important organ of the body. Some people had broken noses, and other people lived with their noses buried in the sand, and yet their bodies kept on living and strutting around with ease.

His fingers trembled on his nose. His nose too was not pointing upwards in that familiar natural position . . . it was pointing downwards. The delicate and tapered tip of his nose was planted on the ground in such a way that his feet were suspended in the air. How could he be standing on the tip of his nose? And how could the delicate and tapered tip of his nose support his body?

Perhaps it was prayer . . . perhaps he had forgotten the motions of prayer . . . it was forty years since he'd last prayed . . . he had been a young child and there had been something called faith . . . but what was there now? This stone building towering in the sky, its thick black shadow cast across the earth, the houses, the buildings, the streets, the cars, the government institutions and the tram lines.

Was time going backwards? Was he reverting to idol worship?

Without doubt, he had fallen into a trap. As he sniffed in exasperation, a few specks of dirt entered his nose. He tried to sneeze and perhaps he did actually sneeze, for someone kicked him in the side. Until that moment, he did not know there were others with him . . . but from the corner of his eye, he noticed a long row of noses, their delicate tips planted on the ground in such a way that their feet were suspended in the air . . .

Another Town, Another Place

Another Town, Another Place

Her hands shut off her ears, for the noise was unbearable, such a noise she had never heard in all her life.
She had heard about something called war, bombs
falling from the sky, houses destroyed, people burned,
everything in ruins. In the cinema she had seen the
rubble of war, had seen explosions and fires. But all that
was just acting, cinema wasn't life and the things that
happened in the cinema couldn't happen in real life or
else why did they make films at all? She used to love
scenes of war on the screen, for they were entertaining
adventures, like adventures of love and sex and other
legends and fables. Life, or at least *her* life, contained no
fables or adventures. She was a respectable woman,
married, had given birth to six legitimate children without knowing either love or sex. Her husband had never
once seen her undressed. When he approached her in
bed, she held him off forcefully and her conscience did

not prick her when she did give in since she had resisted him to the last breath and because she felt no pleasure, but rather pain . . .

The sound of cannon fire resounded. She pressed her hands to her ears and to her skull. God help us, the war is well and truly here! She had not believed there would be war, that a bomb could fall on her house or that she could die or lose an arm or leg. Those horrific things happened in the cinema or to other people. But her? Nothing like that could happen to her. People with disabilities or deformities scared her; she was frightened of corpses covered by sheets. If her husband went away for a few days, her neighbour would come to stay overnight in her apartment. If she went into the bathroom and saw a cockroach scuttling around, she would leave in alarm, particularly if it was one of those large flying types. If she awoke in the middle of the night to the sound of a disturbance in the kitchen, she would curl up under the covers and hide, so that the thief or whoever it was would not notice she was there in the apartment.

The sound of the blast reverberated. Trembling, she ran and hid under the bed. A curse on greed! In Damanhour, we were in our village, people knew us, father earned well. But all his life he was greedy. Patient as a camel for years, he inherited the shop from his father, and kept on telling me: business in Ismailia is worth gold, my brother there has a shop on the canal and nine boys working day and night. The Prophet Mohammed said: 'Share your wealth with your brothers.' She slapped her cheeks in sorrow. My God, we never made a livelihood. They took the boy Mohammed to fight and we married off the five girls to worthless paupers from Damanhour. If only one of them had stayed with me. After six pregnancies and births, I'll die alone like a dog.

She listened from under the bed and, hearing nothing, crept out. No sooner was she on her feet than a bomb exploded somewhere, in the air or on the ground, shaking the walls of the apartment. Umm Mohammed leapt into the wardrobe. God help and protect us. The infidels cannot be victorious over the Muslims. Lord forgive us . . . It's the wrath of God . . . You have the right to be wrathful, Lord. There's no Islam any more, no trust. His brother and his nine sons stole our share in the shop. And he cheated my father in the accounts. I never saw him kneel in prayer. But I ask Your forgiveness, Lord, for Your servants, the Muslims. Sinful as they are they're better than the infidels.

She stuck an ear out of the wardrobe. Everything seemed to be quiet. She crept out cautiously. No sooner had her foot touched the ground than she fell onto her face, clutching her head and ears with her hands. A tremor like an earthquake moved the ground under her feet, the sound of an explosion filled her ears with a sharp whistle. She no longer heard or saw anything.

She came to a minute later and felt her head, shoulders, arms and legs. Everything was in place. She looked up cautiously. The roof was still there above her head. She looked around the room. The walls had not fallen; the wardrobe, the bed, the dressing table, everything was as before. Perhaps it was the sitting room which had collapsed? That would be a catastrophe. The golden suite which her late father had bought for one hundred and sixty pounds. Mrs Tafida and all the neighbours had moved their furniture out two weeks ago. I told him: Let's hire a lorry, Abu Mohammed, and move our furniture. He said to me: Come on old girl, you don't really believe there'll be a war, do you? That's just newspaper talk. All my life I've been hearing about war, but I've never seen it with my own eyes . . .

— So why are people moving their furniture, Abu Mohammed?

— Monkeys imitate each other! It just takes one with an empty head, and they all copy.

She stood up cautiously and craned her neck towards the door to see the entrance to the sitting room. The golden suite must be in pieces by now. What a pity! Nobody but her late father had sat on it.

She walked slowly and carefully to the living room, hands holding her head and blocking her ears. Her eyes scanned the apartment. Thank God, the golden suite was fine, everything was in one piece. One thousand thanks! Her foot stumbled on something on the ground. Oh my God! What is it? Broken glass? She turned in alarm towards the window and found the shutter and the remains of the glass pane and saw the ground covered with small splinters of glass. The window's not ours. It belongs to the landlord. She swallowed hard and went up to the dining table and saw a small piece of something which didn't look like glass. She reached out and picked it up gingerly, held it for a moment, then threw it down in fear. My God, it could be a shrapnel or a bomb or that thing they call napalm!

Time passed and she heard nothing. Everything seemed quiet. She took her hands off her ears and warily opened the shutter. The shop was still in its place at the top of the street. Abu Mohammed was standing in front of it in the centre of a crowd of people, their heads moving here and there looking around, their fingers pointing to something. She followed the direction of their fingers, then screamed in terror. The house of Mrs Tafida, her neighbour, had collapsed. Their house belonged to them. What a disaster! But thank God, Mrs Tafida and her furniture and children had left for Tanta. But where was Mr Hassanain? My God, let's hope he was out of the house! Mr Hassanain, a man of standing at the muncipality.

She put on a black overcoat over her house *galabia* and went out into the street. Noticing her, her husband left the people to come towards her. Scratching his chest, he said:

— Thank God, the shop's in one piece.

— Because the money's clean, Abu Mohammed.

— Cleaner than clean!

— And Mr Hassanain?

— The Lord saved him. He was with me in the shop.

— A worthy man, Abu Mohammed.

— The Lord is with the Muslims.

— And his wife's a worthy woman. She moved her furniture two weeks ago. Why don't we move ours too, Abu Mohammed.

— Move it where?

— To my sister's in Damanhour.

— And from here to Damanhour, how much do you suppose it costs?

— Cost what it may. That golden suite alone is a hundred and sixty pounds. Have you forgotten or what?

— Mr Hassanain says that the muncipality is bringing lorries. I'll go with Mr Hassanain tomorrow and hire one.

143

– Let's go now. Do we know what will happen tomorrow?

Her eyes followed her husband and Mr Hassanain as they walked towards the muncipality, she a few paces behind. More than once her foot stumbled on a piece of brick which had fallen into the street. She noticed a large opening in the wall of a house, small gaps in a veranda. She kissed the tops and palms of her hands in thanks to God when she saw a shop completely destroyed, and turned her face away from a man with blood pouring from his head and some men trying to carry him. God help us . . . is this war? It's not like war in the cinema. She kept her eyes on her husband's back, then looked at Mr Hassanain's. Her husband was short and bent. He had a hump which she'd only ever seen on their wedding night. She thought of the man she'd seen bleeding. Alright, a hump but he was alive. She saw her husband and Mr Hassanain stop. Turning to her, her husband said: Wait for us here, Umm Mohammed.

Umm Mohammed stopped where she was, but looking around she saw a big building with blue windows, surrounded by a large garden with a wire fence on which white jasmine grew. Walking up to the fence to look, she saw a man in a *galabia* holding a hose and watering the flowers . . . There were beds of red, white, yellow and purple flowers. Listening to the spray of the water as it fell onto the flowers, she remembered an incident from her childhood. She had filled a pitcher with water from the sea when suddenly her foot had slipped and the jar had fallen, drenching her head with water. The sound of the water stopped. She looked up to see a man wearing a suit standing with the man in the *galabia* who had been watering the garden. She saw

144

them walk between the flowerbeds and go up to a large one near the fence where she was standing . . . She heard the man in the suit say loudly: I don't like this rose. The man in the *galabia* replied in a soft voice: Why's that, Sir?

— It's too pale. A rose should be true red . . .

She watched the man's pink lips saying: True red . . . the colour of gazelle's blood.

The man with the *galabia* replied: Very well, Sir. The man with the modern suit left and disappeared into the large building. The man in the *galabia* resumed watering the garden.

She put her face to the fence to gaze at the red rose and smell the scent of the jasmine and listen to the spray of the water on the flowers . . . Am I dreaming? Where am I? In what town? She remembered that war had begun an hour or so ago in Ismailia, that she had been at home, had heard the explosions, had see the house of Mr Hassanain destroyed. She remembered all that, but didn't remember having taken a train or bus to this place. Could she have gone from one town to another on foot? It must be the work of the Devil. Could we have taken the train?

She was aroused by a loud voice coming from the garden.

— What are you doing here, my girl?

— Where on earth are we?

— In Ismailia.

— So where was the war an hour or so ago?

The man pointed with his hose towards their street and said: It was there, far away, in Qurshiya. Move away from the fence or you'll get soaked.

She moved away, saw her husband and Mr Hassanain

coming towards her and heard her husband say: The lorry's coming tomorrow. She walked beside him in silence, then suddenly asked him: Are we going back on foot or by train? It seemed to her that her husband stared at her with eyes wide open; but she quietly asked again: Are we going back on foot or are we taking the train?

She Has No Place in Paradise

She Has No Place in Paradise

With the palm of her hand, she touched the ground beneath her but did not feel soil. She looked upwards, stretching her neck towards the light. Her face appeared long and lean, the skin so dark it was almost black.

She could not see her own face in the dark and held no mirror in her hand. But the white light fell onto the back of her hand so that it became white in turn. Her narrow eyes widened in surprise and filled with light. Thus widened and full of light, her eyes looked like those of a *houri*.[1]

In astonishment, she turned her head to the right and to the left. A vast expanse between the leafy trees above her head as she sat in the shade and the stream of water like a strip of silver, its clusters of droplets like pearls, then that deep plate full of broth to the rim.

Her eyelids tightened to open her eyes to the utmost.

149

The scene remained the same, did not alter. She touched her robe and found it to be as soft as silk. From the neck of her gown wafted the scent of musk or good perfume.

Her head and eyes were motionless for she feared that any blink of her eyelids would change the scene or that it would disappear as it had done before.

But from the corner of her eye, she could see the shade stretching endlessly before her, and green trees between the trunks of which she saw a house of red brick like a palace, with a marble staircase leading up to the bedroom.

She remained fixed to the spot, able neither to believe nor disbelieve. Nothing upset her more than the re-currence of the dream that she had died and woken to find herself in paradise. The dream seemed to her impossible, for dying seemed impossible, waking after death even more impossible and going to paradise the fourth impos-sibility.

She steadied her neck still more and from the corner of her eye stared into the light. The scene was still the same, unaltered. The red brick house, like that of the *Omda*, the towering staircase leading to the bedroom, the room itself bathed in white light, the window looking out onto distant horizons, the wide bed, its posts swathed in a curtain of silk, all were still there.

It was all so real it could not be denied. She stayed where she was, fearing to move and fearing to believe. Was it possible to die and waken so quickly and then go to paradise?

What she found hardest to believe was the speed of it all. Death, after all, was easy. Everybody died and her own death was easier than anyone's, for she had lived between life and death, closer to death than to life. When her mother gave birth to her, she lay on top of her with all her weight until she died; her father beat her on the head with a hoe until she died; she had gone into fever after each birth, even until the eighth child; when her husband kicked her in the stomach; when the blows of the sun penetrated under the bones of her head.

Life was hard and death for her was easier. Easier still was waking after death, for no one dies and no one wakens; everyone dies and awakens, except an animal which dies and remains dead.

Her going to paradise was also impossible. But if not her, who would go to paradise? Throughout her life she had never done anything to anger Allah or His Prophet. She used to tie her frizzy black hair with a skein of wool into a plait; the plait she wrapped up in a white headscarf and her head she wrapped in a black shawl. Nothing showed from under her robe except the heel of her foot. From the moment of her birth until her death, she knew only the word: Okay.

Before dawn, when her mother slapped her as she lay, to go and carry dung-pats[2] on her head, she knew only: Okay. If her father tied her to the water mill in place of the sick cow, she said only: Okay. She never raised her eyes to her husband's and when he lay on top of her when she was sick with fever, she uttered only the words: Okay.

She had never stolen or lied in her life. She would go hungry or die of hunger rather than take the food of others, even if it were her father's or brother's or husband's. Her mother would wrap up food for her father in a flat loaf of bread and make her carry it to the field on her head. Her husband's food was also wrapped up in a loaf by his mother. She was tempted, as she walked along with it, to stop under the shade of a tree and open the loaf; but she never once stopped. Each time she was tempted, she

151

called on God to protect her from the Devil, until the hunger became unbearable and she would pick a bunch of wild grass from the side of the road which she would chew like gum, then swallow with a sip of water, filling the cup of her hand from the bank of the canal and drinking until she had quenched her thirst. Then, wiping her mouth on the sleeve of her robe, she would mutter to herself: Thank God, and repeat it three times. She prayed five times a day, her face to the ground, thanking God. If she were attacked by fever and her head filled with blood like fire, she would still praise Allah. On fast days, she would fast; on baking days, she would bake; on harvest days, she would harvest; on holy days, she would put on her mourning weeds and go to the cemetery.

She never lost her temper with her father or brother or husband. If her husband beat her to death and she returned to her father's house, her father would send her back to her husband. If she returned again, her father would beat her and *then* send her back. If her husband took her back and did not throw her out, and then beat her, she returned to her mother who would tell her: Go back, Zeinab. Paradise will be yours in the hereafter.

From the time she was born, she had heard the word 'paradise' from her mother. The first time she'd heard it, she was walking in the sun, a pile of dung on her head, the soles of her feet scorched by the earth. She pictured paradise as a vast expanse of shade without sun, without dung on her head, on her feet shoes like those of Hassanain, the neighbour's son, pounding the earth as he did, his hand holding hers, the two of them sitting in the shade.

When she thought of Hassanain, her imagination went no further than holding hands and sitting in the shade of paradise. But her mother scolded her and told her that neither their neighbour's son Hassanain, nor any other neighbour's son, would be in paradise, that her eyes would not fall on any man other than her father or brother, that if she died after getting married and went to paradise, only her husband would be there, that if her soul was tempted, awake or asleep, and her eye fell on a man other than her husband and even before he held her hand in his, she would not so much as catch a glimpse of paradise or smell it from a thousand metres . . .

From that time, whenever she lay down to sleep, she saw only her husband. In paradise, her husband did not beat her. The pile of dung was no longer on her head; neither did the earth burn the soles of her feet. Their black mud house became one of red brick, inside it a towering staircase, then a wide bed on which her husband sat, holding her hand in his.

Her imagination went no further than holding his hand in paradise. Never once in her life had her hand held her husband's. Eight sons and daughters she had conceived with him without once holding his hand. On summer nights, he lay in the fields; in the winter, he lay in the barn or above the oven. All night long, he slept on his back without turning. If he did turn, he would call to her in a voice like a jackal's: Woman! Before she could answer 'yes' or 'okay', he would have kicked her over onto her back and rolled on top of her. If she made a sound or sighed, he would kick her again. If she did not sigh or make a sound, she would get a third kick, then a fourth until she did. His hand never chanced to hold hers nor his arm happen to stretch out to embrace her.

She had never seen a couple, human or otherwise, embrace except in the dovecot. When she went up there, on the top of the wall appeared a pair of doves, their beaks

153

close together; or when she went down to the cattle pen or from behind the wall there appeared a pair – bull and cow or buffalo or dogs – and her mother brandishing a bamboo stick and whipping them, cursing the animals.

Never in her life had she taken the black shawl off her head nor the white scarf tied under the shawl, except when someone died, when she untied the scarf and pulled the black shawl around her head. When her husband died, she knotted the black shawl twice around her forehead and wore mourning weeds for three years. A man came to ask for her in marriage without her children. Her mother spat in disgust and pulled the shawl down over her forehead, whispering: It's shameful! Does a mother abandon her children for the sake of a man? The years passed by and a man came to ask for her hand in marriage, with her children. Her mother yelled at the top of her voice: What does a woman want in this world after she has become a mother and her husband dies?

One day, she wanted to take off the black shawl and put on a white scarf, but she feared that people would think she'd forgotten her husband. So she kept the black shawl and the mourning weeds and remained sad for her husband until she died of sadness.

She found herself wrapped in a silken shroud inside a coffin. From behind the funeral procession, she heard her mother's wailing like a howl in the night or like the whistle of a train: You'll meet up with your husband in paradise, Zeinab.

Then the noise stopped. She heard nothing but silence and smelled nothing but the soil. The ground beneath her became as soft as silk. She said: It must be the shroud. Above her head, she heard rough voices, like two men fighting. She did not know why they were fighting until

154

she heard one of them mention her name and say that she deserved to go directly to paradise without suffering the torture of the grave. But the other man did not agree and insisted that she should undergo some torture, if only a little: She cannot go directly up to paradise. Everyone must go through the torture of the grave. But the first man insisted that she had done nothing to merit torture, that she had been one hundred percent faithful to her husband. The second man argued that her hair had shown from under her white headscarf, that she had dyed her hair red with henna, that the hennaed heels of her feet had shown from under her robe.

The first man retorted that her hair had never shown, that what his colleague had seen was only the skein of wool, that her robe had been long and thick, under it even thicker and longer underskirts, that no one had seen her heels red.

But his colleague argued, insisting that her red heels had enticed many of the village men.

The dispute between the two of them lasted all night. She lay face down on the ground, her nose and mouth pressed into the earth. She held her breath pretending to be dead. Her torture might be prolonged if it became clear that she had not died; death might save her. She heard nothing of what passed between them; nobody, human or spirit, can hear what happens in the grave after death. If one did happen to hear, one had to pretend not to have heard or not to have understood. The most serious thing to understand is that those two men are not angels of the grave or angels of any type, for it is not possible for angels to ignore the truth which everyone in the village with eyes to see could know: that her heels had never been red like those of the *Omda*'s daughter, but like her face and palms, were always cracked and as black as the soil.

The argument ended before dawn without torture. She thanked God when the voices stopped. Her body grew lighter and rose up as if in flight. She hovered as if in the sky, then her body fell and landed on soft, moist earth and she gasped: Paradise.

Cautiously, she raised her head and saw a vast expanse of green, and thick leafy trees, shade beneath them.

She sat up on the ground and saw the trees stretching endlessly before her. Fresh air entered her chest, expelling the dirt and dust and the smell of dung.

With a slight movement, she rose to her feet. Between the tree trunks she could see the house of red brick, the entrance before her very eyes.

She entered quickly, panting. She climbed the towering staircase panting. In front of the bedroom, she stopped for a moment to catch her breath. Her heart was beating wildly and her chest heaved.

The door was closed. She put out her hand carefully and pushed it. She saw the four posts of the bed, around them a silken curtain. In the middle, she saw a wide bed, on top of it her husband, sitting like a bridegroom. On his right, was a woman. On his left, another woman. Both of them wore transparent robes revealing skin as white as honey, their eyes filled with light, like the eyes of *houris*.

Her husband's face was not turned towards her, so he did not see her. Her hand was still on the door. She pulled it behind her and it closed. She returned to the earth, saying to herself: There is no place in paradise for a black woman.

¹ *houri*: virgin of paradise, according to Islam.
² *dung-pats*: cows' dung is commonly used in Egypt for fuel and in building.

Two Women Friends

Two Women Friends

The sparkle in the black pupil was as it had been for thirty years, as strong and intrusive as daylight. Her arm lifted involuntarily to embrace her. The muscles of her arm contracted, hesitating between a full embrace or leaving a gap, any gap, even one millimetre, to prevent chest touching chest. Her chest was as it had been for thirty years, on it a purple birthmark. The muscles of the small breasts under her white dress were taut and erect, ready to give without reward. Her heart was as open as a naive girl with a childish innocence, whom no man has touched, who has not carried and borne three times, whose eldest son had grown into a man and whose youngest daughter herself had two children.

Thirty years had passed since the two of them had met. If she noticed her somewhere and their eyes almost met, she turned her head away to avoid eye contact. No day had passed without seeing her or lifting the telephone to tell her what had been happening day and night. During term time, no day passed without bringing her head close to hers and whispering the latest news or devilish idea or simple joke. They laughed with suppressed giggles until their chests swelled with air and they almost choked and the imprisoned air involuntarily forced its way out through noses and mouths in intermittent gulps, whereupon the teacher would stop pacing to and fro like a pendulum in front of the blackboard and with slim, pointed fingers like sticks of chalk, would throw them out of the classroom. In the summer holidays, the holiday resort was only a holiday and the travel travel if her friend had come with her. Without her friend, sea, sand, home, school, street, the whole world lost its sparkle and life seemed boring and joyless, with nothing in it except her mother, father, brothers, aunts and uncles. Between all of them and herself, there were no words or conversation. They knew nothing about her other than the results of her end of year exams and the roundness of her body as it developed. Her breasts grew and grew until her chest became the same size as her mother's. Beneath her large chest, no one knew there was a small muscle, the size of a fist, which beat wildly whenever her eyes, through the lattice-holes of the window, fell on the face with its pointed nose and thick black moustache. His name could not cross her lips. Her mother, ear glued to the door of the room which enclosed her and her friend, breathed a sigh of relief at not hearing through the keyhole a man's name pass between them, but only girls' names. At the end of every name, her ears pricked up to catch the last syllable, since the feminine ending on a name turned a boy's name into a girl's name: Amin to Amina, Nabil into Nabila, and so on until the end of the conversation which did not end until the end of the day, the end of the year, the last year of studies, the final exams and then graduation. Then the marriage contract suddenly separated the feminine ending from the last syllable and the name became masculine.

Her arm was still raised involuntarily, its muscles contracted, hesitating between total embrace or leaving a gap between the two chests. Her breasts under the black mourning robe were as large and pendulous as her mother's from which she and her seven siblings had sucked and which were never empty or lacking but always refilled. Her hatred for her mother grew. Since the time she was weaned, it had never happened that her chest had touched her mother's in an embrace. If she returned from travel, the embrace was no more than a handshake or an arm raised to encompass her without holding so that a gap separating her from her mother always remained, and specks the colour of soil swam in the air. In her ear rang a voice as gentle as her father's while she curled up like a foetus on his wide, hairy chest and her head rubbed against his huge neck. Then she would clamber up to touch his thick moustache which exuded the smell of tobacco. He pinched her cheek so that she laughed out loud and she pulled his moustache so that he guffawed revealing nicotine-stained teeth. Her mother looked up from sweeping the floor across the space in which swam specks of dust, over her eyes a layer of grey. Her father whispered gently in her ear: Your mother is jealous of you. The voice stuck in the membrane of her ear and the words ran in her veins, blood corpuscles turning in her brain cells into an idea as solid as lead: Her mother competes with her. She and the woman are rivals.

Her father died before her mother and she was convinced that her mother had killed him. Her eyes were full of accusations towards her, without question, without words, until the last breath leaving her mother's large chest, arm raised to encompass her in a final embrace without touching. Before her eyelids closed for ever, her mother opened her eyes wide and in her open, speechless gaze, she understood the truth. Her eyes widened in understanding, almost as wide as the earth itself and as wide as truth revealed too late. The eyelids dropped for ever and the muscles of her arm struggled to encompass her mother's chest without leaving a gap. But the distance was no longer air. It had grown as thick as a wall. Her mother's chest was no longer a chest but hardened under her hand like a stretch of earth the colour of granite. The paint on the wall in her mother's room disappeared and the bricks, one over the other, grew visible. Over them was a picture of her father wearing something large on his head. On each shoulder, a swelling the size of another shoulder. In each of his gently smiling eyes, another eye without gentleness or a smile.

Her raised arm still encompassed her in a desperate attempt to embrace and to close the gap between the two chests. The other chest stood firm, her heart open, ready to give. But her breasts were large and pendulous, full of guilt and as heavy as the earth. She had lived thirty years hating her mother and hating the large breasts which she had inherited from her. The hatred spread from her chest to the rest of her body and she no longer believed that a man could love her as much as her father had. After her father's death, she married a man whom she hid in her chest year after year. After the wedding, the feminine ending to her name fell away. On his hairy chest, she curled up like a foetus and rubbed her head against his neck to pull his moustache and laugh. She never heard him laugh or even smile and she bore him four boys and a girl without a smile, happiness or pleasure. Even the pleasure of eating and the smell of the morning went and nothing remained but the smell of dust as she swept the floor. On the sofa, her young daughter would rock on his lap or he would make himself into a donkey for her to ride on. Through the rays of the sun carrying specks of dust, her eyes met their four eyes and the laughter stopped, the smiles vanished and a layer of grey covered the six eyes. Since the wedding night, she hated him. Her first son was grown up but she still washed his back with a loofah and soap and thick hair grew as grass on his chest. Every time he went out and returned, she encompassed him with her arm and her large full breasts embraced his chest. In her ears, his father's gruff voice rang: He is no longer a child. He's a mule. Her son replied inaudibly: There's no mule here but you.

The grey hair stood over the upper lip, revealing decayed and nicotine-stained teeth. The large palm lifted into the air, undecided whether to land on the face of the son or of the mother. Before the grey hair replaced the black hair, the palm used to land on the face of the child. But the child grew into a man and was twice the height of his father. The huge palm no longer hesitated to land on the face of the mother.

During every slap, her hand lifted in the air, contracted muscles hesitant and undecided whether to land on his face or on the face of one of her four sons or the little girl. Each time her hand landed on the face of the girl. She was the smallest and weakest and above all, she was only a girl. At night, she slept beside him as if nothing had happened. He reached out to embrace her as if nothing had happened. In the morning, she made him tea as if nothing had happened. He left for work as usual and returned at noon. She left for work as usual after he left. She returned before he did and he found she had already swept the floor, washed and cooked.

Her arm still reached out to encompass the two chests together, her muscles contracted unable to eliminate the gap between the chests, the eye unable to stare into the eye, but the sparkle in the black pupil was still as strong as daylight, as it had been for thirty years. Around the eyes and the mouth, lines like wrinkles, but the face was still as taut as string. The chest beat under the small, firm breasts. The muscles of her back were tense and beat under her arm like a heart. Warmth, like the flame of youth, ran through the blood from her arm to her shoulder and back and all the muscles of her body beat and left her year after year after year for thirty years to return as she had been, a pupil in class. The chronic pain in the back of her head eased and the weight of her body, of her head on her neck, of her neck on her back, of her chest on her heart and everything in her grew lighter, even her large, cumbersome breasts shrank and rose above the ribs with taut muscles. The closed air canals in her heart opened and the air rushed from her nose and mouth to her chest like intermittent gasps. Her arm reached out further and her muscles contracted in a desperate attempt to eliminate the gap. The fixed idea in the brain was like a ball of copper. Everything in her life changed, except this idea. Her body changed, the features of her face changed, the colour of her eyes changed, the shape of her muscles and her movement across the ground, even the ground itself changed. The cells of the brain under her skull changed into other cells. Only this idea remained like a ball of copper, the size of a pinhead, moving a little from the back of the head to the front, or from left to right, or right to left, but remaining the same, unchanging.

Her arm was still raised to encompass her. A gap of no more than one millimetre still separated the two chests. Her head rubbed the slender neck, the pulse in it beating like the heart of a mother. The blood ran from her neck to her back and her spine and rose again to her head to hit against the rusty copper ball. She stuck her nose into the neck to smell the tobacco. Her hand almost reached out to pull the moustache on the upper lip, but her fingers contracted above the smooth, hairless skin. The smell of lilac filled her chest instead of tobacco. Above her stretched out arm, she saw the wall without paint, on it the face of her father inside a black frame, a line as deep as a trench on the wide forehead. Under the trench, two eyes staring at her, like those of her husband. Thirty years she had lived with him, in one bed, without seeing his eyes. Year after year, day after night, she had not looked at his face. She left for work in the morning as usual after he had left and returned at the end of the day before he returned. As usual, she swept, washed and cooked.

Once, out of the usual, she returned from work early to find him in her bed with his arm around another woman. His back was turned towards her and she did not see his face. Facing her was the chest of the other woman. The muscles of the small breasts were firm and erect, ready to give without return, a purple birthmark on the chest and heart.

The muscles of her arm were still contracted in a desperate attempt to eliminate the picture engraved in the back of the head. Time, like a black cloud, hung over the eye. The pain, like a deep trench, in the heart. Her husband went away, died and then returned, over his head a long shawl like a woman's veil covering him from head to toe, his eyes on the wall staring at her without a smile, like her father's eyes. On the wide forehead, a line as deep as a trench. Her arm still attempted to surround in a final embrace. A gap still remaining between one chest and the other, the air as thick as the wall on which there was a crack as deep as a wound. But the sparkle in the black pupil was still as strong as daylight and on her chest was a purple birthmark. Her heart was open, ready to give without return and the blood rushed from the heart to the head. In the rush of blood, the piece of rust dislodged from the brain cells and was washed by the blood. Over the eye, time melted away like a veil washed by tears. Chest embraced chest without a gap, head met head like in schooldays. Their breath was suppressed until their chests were full of air and almost choked. The imprisoned air rushed through the nostrils and the mouth involuntarily in the form of intermittent gulps, as two children laughing and crying. The open eye in the crack in the wall stared at them and laughter took over from crying.

'Beautiful'

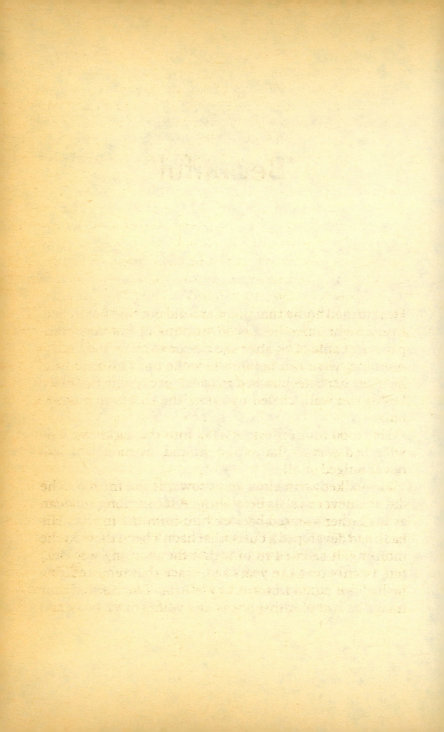

'Beautiful'

He returned home that night and did not find her in bed. Every night since he'd been working in the new company, he came back after she'd gone to sleep and, in the morning, went out before she woke up. This morning, he'd left her asleep in bed as usual, occupying the place beside the wall, curled up under the sheets in a white bulge.

He stood motionless, staring into the darkness. The wide bed was as flat as the ground, as though it had never bulged at all.

He walked with slow steps towards the mirror as he did whenever a crisis befell him. A face as long and lean as his father's stared back at him from the mirror. His back had developed a curve that hadn't been there in the morning. It seemed to him that the morning was one, ten, twenty or more years ago; since that remote time, he had not stood in front of a mirror. The most recent image he had of himself was as a young man, body and muscles taut, head held high and back straight. His arms, when he clasped them around himself, enveloped the universe; and at night, he enveloped her as if she were the universe.

She was with him in the same company in Old Cairo. Their life stretched out before them filled with an orange sunlit glow. And his arms, when he clasped them around himself, enveloped the universe. He possessed the universe and possessed her when he enveloped her. The delight of possession had a pungent taste and tangible presence for him.

He possessed nothing but the universe and her. When his father died, he inherited nothing but his picture in a frame, engraved in his mind and hung on the wall. In the picture, his father was standing to receive a medal, wearing evening dress, his hand outstretched, his head bowed with the curve of his back.

He had never seen his father bowed before. When he stood up, he appeared tall, proud, his back firm, his head high. When his schoolmates bragged about their fathers and the possessions they had, he bragged that he had a father whose head and back bowed to no one.

His friends, in that distant time, did not brag about their mothers. None of them so much as mentioned his mother's name. But in his heart of hearts, he was proud of her, for she knew no man other than his father and only stopped working and moving when carried on the bier. Her voice was a whisper and was never raised; her footsteps on the ground were inaudible apart from the rustle of her robe. If she sneezed aloud, she would clasp her hand over her nose and beg pardon.

Like his father, his mother had died on her feet. Neither did she sleep. When she lay on the bed, she

170

occupied only a small space next to the wall the size of her body. When his father came home, she got up and did not sleep until he did. She also did not die until he died. Then she gathered up his clothes and put them in a wooden box under the bed. In the middle of the box lay his evening dress, the medal pinned onto the breast, small white mothballs all around it.

He closed his eyes, then opened them to find himself still standing before the mirror, wearing evening dress like his father's, on his breast a disc shining like a medal. His face was as pale as his father's when he died. Behind him, the bed remained as flat as the ground, as though it had never bulged at all, as though she had never slept in it. Every night she used to lie on her right side, back towards him and face to the wall, curled up just like his mother when she slept, arms clasped to her chest, legs clasped to her stomach, head covered so that nothing of her showed.

Her sleeping body assured him of her eternal faithfulness to him and filled him with such self-confidence that, in his heart of hearts, he would almost have been as proud of her as of his mother – were it not for what happened.

He shut his eyes as he stood before the mirror. Her image vanished from his mind and he forgot what had happened. But then he remembered, and forgot, one hundred times, one thousand times. He remembered, then forgot, then remembered. He saw her before him, not asleep in bed but sitting, not with him or with her brother or father or any male member of the family or of the area or even the country, but with a foreign man, a complete foreigner, who knew not one word of Arabic.

She never had liked her red nylon gown and preferred

171

rather the sky-blue cotton one, with its white embroidery in the form of jasmine. It was the one she had worn for him alone, the sparkle in her eyes with him alone, before the wedding. After the wedding, the sparkle came and went, and then disappeared. He did not know how it had gone, but since that time, he had been anxious and a sort of suspicion came and went, then came. As soon as he noticed the sparkle return to her eyes, he would look around apprehensively and if he noticed a window open or half open, he would imagine a man behind it.

He was still in the small apartment in Old Cairo. The houses were cramped together; the neighbour's windows remained either open or closed throughout the day. Only one window stayed half open or half closed, the shutter old and worn, the face peering from behind it old and worn. But it was a man's face and, in his opinion, a man did not stand at the window unless he were peering out at woman.

She did not stand at the window except on her day off, the one day in the week she did not go to the company. The window was small, the glass broken and blocked with wood. The surrounding walls allowed only a thin ray of sunlight to steal in before sunset which fell onto the wall near the window ledge. Her outstretched hands could touch the ray before it vanished. In the winter, the ray felt warm and orange and was reflected in her eyes, the light appearing like a sparkle. When he saw the sparkle, he glanced around him anxiously, seeing neither the sun nor the ray, nothing except that half open or closed window, imagining that it stayed that way to allow the person behind it to see without being seen.

His voice, like his father's, would rise when he got angry at the slightest thing. But nothing about her used to anger him, for she, like his mother, did not stop working, inside and outside the house. Her movements, like those of his mother, were soundless; her voice a whisper, was never raised. If he raised his voice in anger, she remained silent and did not answer back. But the one thing that did make him angry was seeing her stand at the window. In his heart of hearts, he knew she was like his mother and that she knew no man other than him; but, like his father, he did not know love without suspicion and could not imagine a woman standing at the window watching only the sun.

Once, he hit her to make her close the window and she closed it. A week went by, her day off came, and he saw her open it. He hit her again, more forcefully than the previous time. He believed that the force of his beating reflected the force of his jealousy and that the force of his jealousy reflected the force of his love and that she should be happy, like his mother when his father had beaten her. But she was not happy.

She was not happy when he bought her the red nylon gown and she continued to prefer the old blue cotton one. When they moved to the large flat in Ma'adi he did not see her happy. When his salary doubled and he made her stay at home, she was not happy. When 'Uncle Othman' came and she no longer had to cook or wash or clean, she showed no signs of happiness or contentment.

He opened his eyes to find himself still standing in front of the mirror, his face as long and lean as his father's, with the same bent back, his evening suit like his father's, on the breast a round disc gleaming like a medal. It was not metallic but made of green cloth, on which white letters of nylon shone: *Transnational*.

The letters looked strange, written in a foreign language, as if he had never seen them before, as if he were discovering the badge on his breast for the first time. He was wearing the name of the new company. He had been going there every day for the last ten years and, in all that time, had not looked at himself in the mirror. Time was short, every moment had its price and was registered by computer. He received his salary in dollars, his desk had a baize top, on it a telephone with a recall that memorized numbers with buttons that almost worked themselves before being touched, and the glass in the window was imported, of the smoked kind which allowed one to look out without being seen, and the neon light was as bright as ten lamps.

When she sat in the light, her red nylon robe shimmered, gathered at the neck in a ruffle as fine as an ants' nest, narrowing at the waist under a wide velvet belt, then swirling around her thighs like folds of lotus leaves.

Beautiful!

The word, spoken in a foreign language, rang in his ears as if he were hearing it for the first time, discovering its meaning for the first time, understanding what it meant and that the person saying it was a man, a man who was not her husband nor her brother nor her father nor any male member of the family or quarter or even country, but a completely foreign man, his face pink, his nose large and curved, over his eyes a pair of reflecting sunglasses through which he could see everything without anyone seeing his eyes.

She was sitting in front of him wearing her red nylon

robe. For the first time, he realized that it was transparent. He was sitting in front of her, looking at her, seeing her. More serious than just seeing, he was discovering her beauty; and more serious than this discovery, he was expressing it aloud. And she was sitting in front of him, listening to him, getting neither angry nor excited. Neither did she seem to be annoyed, but remained seated, nodding as if she were happy, saying aloud, in English: Thank you.

Sitting in front of her, he understood she was thanking him. She remained seated, neither rising nor getting angry. He remained seated in front of her, flirting with her. For him, telling a woman that she was beautiful was flirting. And she was not just any woman, but his wife. And he was not just any husband, but a man as tough as his father, who permitted no one to see her, even from behind the shutter, let alone face to face, or shake hands with her, or flirt with her aloud, while he sat in front of him and did not get up and hit him or her, or at least protest and show his anger. No, he just sat there without protesting, no sign of annoyance on his face. Whenever his eyes met theirs, he nodded and smiled.

He opened his eyes to find himself still before the mirror. He was still smiling, but his face was as lean and pale as his father's when he died. The curve of his back was even greater than before and he tensed his muscles to hide it. But it was not hidden and remained visible. He also tensed his face muscles, trying to hide the smile; but it too did not disappear. He moved his feet to get up and go, but could not move. She too remained seated. He expected her to get up and go, but she did neither and remained sitting, nodding and saying, in English: Thank you.

The words pierced his ears like an arrow, as material evidence planted in his head, affirming her eternal treachery to him, as though she had betrayed him all along, after he had married her, before he had married her, since her very existence on earth, since the earth's very existence.

Her treachery came as a surprise, like the first slap on his face. He expected himself to return it with a more forceful one. His large hand rose into the air, then shook a little in hesitation. It almost felt onto his face or onto that of his father, but once again he remembered her treachery and, angry both with himself and with his father, his large palm fell onto her face.

He opened his eyes suddenly to find himself still standing in front of the mirror. His face was still long and lean like his father's but it had divided into two long and lean faces, a deep horizontal line between them. His right hand was stretched out in front of him, on it a thin thread the colour of blood.